domain.456

Self-esteem
Differences
Authority

Bev Gundersen and Linda Kondracki

NEXGEN®

Building the New Generation of Believers

An Imprint of Cook Communications Ministries
Colorado Springs, Colorado

domain.456: Self-esteem, Differences, Authority

Series Editor: Ellen Larson
Interior Design: Jeff Jansen
Illustrated by: Sonny Carder

Published by Cook Communications Ministries
4050 Lee Vance View
Colorado Springs, CO 80918-7100
www.CookMinistries.com/NexGen

Colorado Springs, Colorado/Paris, Ontario

Printed in the United States of America

ISBN: 0-7814-5518-9

Table of Contents ☑

Welcome to the Junior Electives Series

Let's talk about it ...

What is it like to grow up in America today? How do our Junior-age children perceive the world around them, and their place in it? Did you know that your Junior students are more aware of the world around them than any previous generation of American children? However, seen through their eyes the world is often seen as a scary and anxious place. Every day they are blatantly confronted with the threat of nuclear disasters, ecological concerns that warn them their planet may not exist by the time they grow up, and an increasing number of their classmates either wielding knives and guns at school or killed in gang-related incidents. Closer to home, you can expect a high number of your students to have experienced at least one divorce in their family, or suffered some kind of physical, sexual, or emotional abuse from family members.

As adults, we may like to close our eyes and see the days of childhood as carefree and innocent as they might have been in our day. But when we open our eyes and see the world as our kids see it today, it is clear that life holds much stress and anxiety for our children. Instead of wishing for simpler days, it is time for us to say to our kids, "Let's talk about it . . ."

The Junior Electives Series was designed to help you do just that. Each topic in the series was selected because it represents issues Juniors are concerned about, and in many cases learning about from their peers, the media, or in school. With the help of this curriculum, you will be able to provide an opportunity for them to discuss their concerns in a Christian context. For many of your kids, this may be the first chance they will have to hear that the Bible has a lot to teach them about each of these contemporary life concerns.

As you teach the lessons in this series, you will have an opportunity to:
• Introduce and teach topics of concern to Juniors in a distinctively Christian context.
• Provide a safe place to learn about, talk about, and express feelings about each issue.

• Teach practical skills and biblical principles Juniors can use to cope with each concern in their daily lives.
• Provide a tool to help parents facilitate family discussion and coping in the home setting.

Features of the Junior Elective Series

Four-Part Lesson Plan

Each lesson follows this format:

1. Setting the Stage (5-10 minutes). Each lesson begins with an activity designed to do two things. First, it is a gathering activity, meaning that you can involve your students in it as soon as they arrive. You do *not* need to have the whole class present to begin your lesson time. By arriving early and having the Setting the Stage activity set up and ready for the kids as soon as they walk in the door, you will communicate a sense of excitement about the lesson and set a tone of orderliness for your class.

Second, the Setting the Stage activity is purposeful in that it will draw the students into the subject for the day. It is more than just something to keep the kids busy while everyone arrives. The activity will provide a fun and interesting way to draw the kids' attention to an area of interest in their lives. Most of the time, it will also raise questions which will lead them into the next section of the lesson.

2. Introducing the Issue (20 minutes). Building on the Setting the Stage activity, this section of the lesson will involve the kids in an active discussion of the topic of the day. The material provided for you contains information the kids need to know, anticipating key questions they may have. It also includes one or more learning activities particularly designed to encourage your students to talk about the issues most on their minds, while in the context of a Christian community. To make this time as effective as possible, you will need to establish your class as a safe place where everyone's feelings and questions are welcomed and treated seriously (some suggestions for doing that are listed on page 5). Once that has been accomplished, you may be surprised at how much your Juniors have to say, and the depth of their thinking!

3. Searching the Scriptures (20 minutes). This section of each lesson takes your class to the Bible to discover what God has to say about the topic being discussed. Your students may be amazed to find out just how much the Bible says about subjects that seem so *modern*. Through a wide variety of creative teaching methods, your class will study people and principles of Scripture that speak directly to the concerns gripping their hearts and minds. As you study together, you will also be acquainting them with the most valuable resource they can have for coping with these contemporary issues: their Bibles.

4. Living the Lesson (5-10 minutes). The final section of each lesson challenges the kids to take what they've learned and apply it to their own lives. It's the *so what* section. The class members will be encouraged to ask themselves, "So what am I going to do with what I've just learned?"

Clearly Stated Key Principles

Each book in the Junior Electives Series contains three units, each of which addresses a different topic of concern. The following three unit features will help your students focus on and remember the central principles of each unit.

1. Unit Verse. One verse has been chosen for each unit that summarizes the biblical principle central to the unit topic. The meaning of this verse is developed a little more each week as students work on a cooperative learning activity designed to help them understand and apply a key biblical principle.

2. Unit Affirmation. The primary learning objective for each unit has been phrased into an affirmation sentence that begins with "I can . . . " Discussing this affirmation each week will empower your students by letting them know they can do something positive about issues that may feel frightening or overwhelming.

3. Unit Service Projects. At the end of each unit you will find several ideas for your class not only to learn about the unit issue, but actually DO something about it. Although they are optional, taking the extra time to involve your class in a unit project will help them practice new skills and see for themselves that they can take an active role in the issues that affect their lives.

Parent Informational Letter

At the beginning of each unit, you will find PART-NERS . . . , a newsletter that you can photocopy and send home to the parents of your class members. This letter gives parents an overview of the topic being studied, as well as some practical ideas of ways they can further their child's learning through several Do-At-Home activities.

Flexibility and Variety

The Junior Electives Series has been designed to be usable in any number of settings. It is equally effective in a Sunday-school setting, a Wednesday-night series, or even a special setting such as a weekend retreat. If you live in an area that participates in release time, this series is an exellent resource to present biblical principles in a contemporary way. Feel free to be creative and find the best place for your group to talk about these important life principles.

A variety of learning activities are used to present the issue information and biblical truths. The following materials are considered standard supplies and are recommended to be available for the classtimes:

- Bibles
- Glue
- Tape
- Pencils
- Scissors
- Stapler
- Paper

A Word about Children and Stress . . .

As you prepare to teach the Junior Electives Series, it is important to realize that many of the subjects you will be studying are the sources of stress in the lives of your students. Many students may never have had the chance to talk openly about these issues, and doing so in your class may well raise their anxiety level. Throughout these sessions, there are several things you can keep in mind:

1) Point them to Jesus. Perhaps the greatest benefit of the Junior Elective Series is that it will give you the opportunity to help your kids learn that a relationship to Jesus Christ is the best resource we can have to face the stressful, anxious parts of our lives. Through the Bible studies and your own personal witness of the power of Christ in your life, you can have the privilege of introducing children to Jesus and inviting them to ask Him to be an active part of their lives.

2) Create a safe place where they can talk about their real feelings. Children have a strong tendency to say the things in class that they think teachers want to hear. Early on in this series, you will want to create a safe place for sharing by continually reassuring your kids that they can say what is really on their minds, and making a rule that no one can criticize or make fun of anything anyone else shares in class. In many cases, expressing their feelings in a safe place, and having those feelings accepted by you and the class will relieve much of their anxiety.

3) If necessary, help them get outside help. You may find a child in your class who is experiencing an unusual amount of stress. In that case, ask your pastor or Christian Education Director for the procedure your church uses to refer children and families for professional help.

Celebrating ME!

The phrase "self-esteem" has become a buzzword in the last decade. School curriculum is developed to boost it, parents are warned not to damage it, and entire books are devoted to instructing us how to raise self-esteem. In the book *The New Peoplemaking*, by Virginia Satir, self-esteem is defined as "the ability to value one's self and to treat oneself with dignity, love, and reality."

The feelings and ideas we develop about ourselves certainly play a significant role in how we act, feel and relate to others. It's easy to identify a child who does not have high self-esteem! But the good news for Christians is that God created each one of us and we can be sure that He is pleased with His creation! You may have heard the popular phrase "God doesn't make junk." Genesis 1:31 affirms that statement when it says "God saw all that he had made, and it was very good."

In the weeks ahead, you will have the opportunity to take your students to God's Word and help them see how God created each of them as a unique individual. As they review the Unit Verse each week, they will be challenged to accept God's affirmation when He said "You are precious and honored in my sight, and . . . I love you" (Isaiah 43:4). In response they are able to say "I can like myself." What a gift to pass on to your class members!

Self-esteem Overview

Unit Verse: You are precious and honored in my sight, and . . . I love you. Isaiah 43:4
Unit Affirmation: I CAN LIKE MYSELF!

LESSON	TITLE	OBJECTIVE	SCRIPTURE BASE
Lesson #1	Fit for a King	That your students will understand that God created them as unique individuals and places great value on them.	Jeremiah 1:4-10
Lesson #2	I Approve!	That your students will accept themselves the way God created them and not compare themselves to others.	Judges 6:1-16
Lesson #3	Sticks and Stones . . .	That your students will avoid letting the opinions of others affect how they feel about themselves.	Genesis 6:5-15, 22
Lesson #4	Talking to Myself	That your students will avoid thinking and talking negatively about themselves but instead, with God's help, build themselves up in positive ways.	I Timothy 4:12-16a
Lesson #5	Awesome Adolescence	That your students will understand and accept physical and emotional changes as normal parts of God's plan for growing up.	Psalm 139:1-4, 13, 14

Partners

For the next few weeks your Junior-age child will be part of a group learning about Self-esteem. *Partners* is a planned parent piece to keep you informed of what will be taught during this exciting series.

PREVIEW...

Self-esteem

We hear the word "self-esteem" many places in today's world. In fact, it has become a buzzword in the last decade. School curriculum has been developed to boost it, parents are warned not to damage it, and entire books are devoted to instructing us how to improve and raise self-esteem. Within the Christian community, however, there are many who feel that our society is too self-centered and the term "self-esteem" should have little or no place in the life of the Christian. Yet the phrase "Love your neighbor as yourself" appears over nine times in the Bible. Traditionally, we have focused on the phrase "love your neighbor" while downplaying the "love yourself" part of this commandment. The important concept we miss when we do this, is that we cannot love others in healthy ways until we know what it means to love ourselves in God-honoring

ways. The pattern of how to love others is how we love ourselves.

In the book *The New Peoplemaking,* by Virginia Satir, self-esteem is defined as "the ability to value one's self and to treat oneself with dignity, love, and reality." If we accept this definition of self-esteem and combine it with God's command, then the intent of God's command to "love others as we love ourselves" becomes powerfully real. Simply stated, persons with good self-esteem are able to treat themselves with dignity, love, and a clear sense of what is real. Out of this ability, then, grows the ability to treat others with the same love and esteem. What an important gift to give our children!

During this unit, these concepts are explored and reinforced as the kids study God's Word and discover how God created them as unique individuals. As they review the Unit Verse each week, they will be challenged to accept God's affirmation when He said "You are precious and honored in My sight, and . . . I love you." In response to God's view of them, they will affirm "I can like myself."

Unit Verse:

You are precious and honored in my sight, and . . . I love you. Isaiah 43:4

Unit Affirmation:

I CAN LIKE MYSELF!

PRINCIPLES...

Self-esteem

PRINCIPLE #1:
GOD CREATED ME AS A UNIQUE INDIVIDUAL, LOVES ME, AND VALUES ME.

The feelings and ideas we develop about ourselves certainly play a significant role in how we act, feel, and relate toward others. The good news for Christians is that God created each one of us and we can be sure that He is pleased with His creation. You may have heard the popular phrase "God doesn't make junk." Genesis 1:31 backs up that statement when it says "God saw all that he had made, and it was very good."

This is a particularly important concept for your Juniors since they are approaching a time in their lives when it is important to "be like everybody else." In a society that places value on wearing the right clothes, looking the right way, and saying the right things, the subject of being unique is not very popular. One way for you to help your child prepare for this time is by reinforcing the value of being the unique person God created him or her to be.

PRINCIPLE #2:
THE OPINIONS OF THOSE AROUND ME MATTER LESS THAN GOD'S OPINION OF ME.

The opinions and attitudes of the people around us can affect the way we act and feel about ourselves regardless of our age. We do care about what others think of us. For kids, this issue is especially important. Our task as parents and teachers is to help our kids learn to value God's opinion of us as the most important and then to identify when it is necessary to let the opinions of others go.

Looking at the life of Noah, your kids will see an example of someone who had to do just that. Noah no doubt endured much criticism and ridicule for consistently maintaining a close walk with God. His obedience to the strange directions to build a huge boat in the middle of the desert brought even more alienation. But the opinions of the people around Noah changed drastically when the rain started to fall. In the long run, God's opinion is the one that matters most! We can be sure that He loves us and plans only the best for us.

PRINCIPLE #3:
WHAT I THINK AND SAY ABOUT MYSELF IS IMPORTANT.

Every day, each of us receives thousands of messages about who we are and what we are like. These messages come from sources such as parents, teachers, television, and peers. The process of receiving and interpreting these messages is called "self-talk." The information we accept and believe can greatly influence how we feel

about ourselves. When we put ourselves down we are criticizing one of God's most precious creations. When we allow our thoughts to dwell on the negative it soon becomes hard to see the good. Because we are created in God's image, we need to see ourselves from His perspective. Here again, the Unit Verse is an important affirmation for your kids to embrace.

PRINCIPLE #4:
GOD HAS A SPECIAL PLAN FOR MY GROWTH AND FUTURE.

Growing up presents a variety of challenges! As kids begin to mature and change, feelings of awkwardness and inferiority can seem overwhelming. We can help by reminding our kids that God has a special plan for each of them and it includes growing, changing, and experiencing exciting new opportunities and accomplishments in the days ahead!

PRACTICE...
Self-esteem
1. DO A SELF CHECKUP.

How do you feel about yourself? It's difficult to pass something on to our children when we haven't experienced it

for ourselves. Take some time to evaluate your own feelings of self-worth. Could they be improved? If so, read a book about the subject, talk to a friend or pastor and ask the Lord to help you in this area. Both you and your child will benefit from it!

2. MEMORIZE THE UNIT VERSE.

Make this a family project. There is no greater power for raising self-esteem than to be reminded that the great God of our universe sees us as precious and lovely. He regards us with honor!

3. BE AN ENCOURAGER.

The world is full of critics! Be an encourager to your child. Look for the positives in each life and vocalize thanksgiving and encouragement for them. Affirm your child for who and what he or she is—a gift from God and a unique individual. Use phrases such as: I like the way you..., It was great when you . . . , Thanks for . . . , I'm so proud of the way you . . . , You made a super choice when . . . . Remind your child daily of your love.

4. DESIGN A SPECIAL CELEBRATION.

During the next few weeks, pick a special time to honor each person in your family. Mealtimes work especially well. Recognize the "honoree" by preparing a favorite meal. Create a special place setting at the table. Have others in the family write notes or cards to tell what is most special to them about the honoree. Read the cards at the end of the meal. Celebrate the things that make that person special and unique from anyone else in the family.

Fit for a King

Aim: That your students will understand that God created them as unique individuals and places great value on them.

Scripture: Jeremiah 1:4-10

Unit Verse: You are precious and honored in my sight, and . . . I love you. Isaiah 43:4

Unit Affirmation: I CAN LIKE MYSELF!

✔ Planning Ahead

1. Photocopy Activity Sheets (pages 15 and 16)—one for each student. Cut page 15 into two sections (1 and 2).
2. Prepare one set of three lunch bags for every four to five students. Label the bags as follows: #1 ANIMALS ONLY, #2 BOTH ANIMALS AND HUMANS, #3 HUMANS ONLY.
3. Prepare the Unit Affirmation poster by writing across the top of a large poster board "I CAN LIKE MYSELF." Under the title, write the numbers 1-5 vertically down the left-hand side.
4. Have available several of the following fingerprinting supplies: inked stamp pads, paper, paper towels, and magnifying glasses.
5. Write the phrase "THANK YOU GOD FOR ME" on a three–foot long paper. Attach it to the wall at an appropriate height for students to write or draw on.

1 Setting the Stage (5-10 minutes)

WHAT YOU'LL DO

- Participate in a sorting activity to emphasize that humans are unique and special

WHAT YOU'LL NEED

- "Created Unique!" Activity Sheet (page 15)
- Sets of lunch bags

2 Introducing the Issue (20 minutes)

WHAT YOU'LL DO

- Discuss ways God created human beings as unique and different from all other creation
- Play a movement game to reinforce our uniqueness
- Prepare a fingerprint gallery to examine each person's individual uniqueness
- Introduce the Unit Affirmation poster

WHAT YOU'LL NEED

- "Created Unique!" Activity Sheet (page 15)
- Fingerprinting supplies
- Unit Affirmation poster

3 Searching the Scriptures (20 minutes)

WHAT YOU'LL DO

- Explore how God called and enabled a young man to His special messenger to the people
- Use an activity sheet to discover God's promises to us as His special, unique individuals

WHAT YOU'LL NEED

- "You Can Bank On It!" Activity Sheet (page 16)

4 Living the Lesson (5-10 minutes)

WHAT YOU'LL DO

- Celebrate our uniqueness by affirming each other's strengths

WHAT YOU'LL NEED

- A banner labeled "THANK YOU GOD FOR ME"
- Completed fingerprint names

Lesson 1

Setting the Stage (5-10 minutes)

Before your students arrive today, create several identical activity stations. Place copies of the top half of the activity sheet "Created Unique!" (page 15), scissors, Bibles, and a set of paper bags at each station. As the children enter the room, explain they are to cut apart the statements on the activity sheet, read each statement or look up the Scripture reference and then place the paper in the bag which best describes the statement: ANIMALS ONLY, BOTH ANIMALS AND HUMANS, HUMANS ONLY. After all have arrived and finished the activity, review their findings.

What are some things humans and animals have in common? (Both made by God, all statements in the "Both" bag.) **Why wasn't God satisfied with a world containing only plants and animals?** (There was no one to communicate with. He wanted someone to talk with and enjoy.) **Why did God create human beings?** (To be a friend, and share a relationship.) **Name some things that make humans different from animals.** Refer to items in the "Humans Only" bag.

Our God is a God of variety. There are hundreds of different species of animals. Each is different and has its own characteristics and peculiarities. People are just as different. God has created each one of us according to His plan, and as unique individuals. The word "unique" means "being the only one." In the next few weeks, we will be learning how very special and unique each of us is. Be prepared! You will probably discover some new things to celebrate about yourself!

Introducing the Issue (20 minutes)

Let's take a few minutes to see how different we really are! As I read the following statements move to the right side of the room if the statement is true about you, and the left side if it is not true. Select statements from the following list or make up some of your own:

I LIKE:
- green beans better than broccoli
- pizza better than hamburgers
- teddy bears more than snakes
- baseball better than soccer
- reading more than math
- the color blue more than pink
- Coke better than Pepsi

- chocolate better than vanilla

As we moved, you saw an excellent example of how we all have very specific likes and dislikes. No two people like all the same things. God designed each one of us to be a unique person in our likes, dislikes, hobbies, looks, and millions of other ways. What are some other ways that we, in our class, are different from each other? Let kids respond by telling each other about their hobbies, activities, families, unique interests, and experiences.

It is important to remind ourselves that it is good to be different and unique from everyone else, especially during those times when we want to be "just like everyone else." We may wish we could throw the ball as well as "everyone else" on our baseball team, or wear the same kind of clothes as "everyone else" in our class. Sometimes our society tries to tell us that being different is not good! During those times when we feel that we just have to be like everyone else, we can remember one very important point: no one else in all the world is just like me! Don't ever forget that no one can fill your place in the world; no one can give joy to the people who love you like you do; and if you were gone from our world, absolutely no one in all the world could ever take your place! Be sure all your kids understand this point before moving on. Kids this age are very fearful about feeling different. They need to be reassured that they can celebrate their uniqueness as a gift from God and make it a source of high (not low!) self-esteem!

Explain to your students that every day they carry with them a guarantee of the fact that no one could ever take their place. Even though there are billions of people in our world, and we are all humans, there are things about each of us that are different from anyone else in the world: one is the DNA in the cells of our bodies. Another is our fingerprints! Although everyone has fingerprints, no two are exactly the same. Even identical twins have different fingerprints. The skin covering our fingertips is full of ridges arranged in intricate patterns. These patterns stay the same throughout a person's lifetime. The only way they can ever change is by surgery, disease or an accident. During the 1880s, a British anthropologist calculated mathematically that it could be possible for no two persons to have the same exact fingerprint patterns. Of course, as the One who made us, God knew this all along. Then in the 1890s, two police officers created a system to categorize fingerprints. Today we use computers to classify and compare prints and have discovered that every fingerprint belongs to one of four major categories: loop, whorl, arch, or accidental. There are also eight subclassifications of the main types of patterns.

Distribute the Fingerprint Classification portion of the activity sheet "Created

Unique!" (page 15), paper, paper towels, inked stamp pads and the magnifying glasses. Instruct the students to "print" their unique identity on paper using their fingerprints and then use a magnifying glass to examine them closely. **Using the Classification sheet, can you identify any of the major patterns in your own fingerprints? Are all your fingers the same?** As time allows, encourage the kids to compare their prints to others in the class. Set the prints aside to dry for use later.

Display the Unit Affirmation poster where all can see it. Read it aloud together. **It is surprising how many kids really don't like themselves very much. Although we all have things about ourselves we don't like, God invites us to see ourselves as the special and unique persons He created us to be. What have we learned so far today that can help us like ourselves more?** Let kids suggest some phrases that can be added to the first line. Possibilities include: "By celebrating my uniqueness," or, "by thanking God for making me different from everyone else." Choose one and write it on the first line. **Now let's take a look at someone in the Bible who had some trouble liking himself, too.**

✓ Searching the Scriptures (20 minutes)

Ask students to find Jeremiah chapter one in their Bibles. **Who was Jeremiah?** (A prophet) **Imagine for a moment what it must have been like for Jeremiah to have been visited by God and called to be a prophet. One day you are just going about your business, when you hear the voice of God speaking to you. He tells you some incredible things about choosing you to be His spokesperson to kings and rulers. How do you think Jeremiah felt at that moment? Do you think he was glad to be chosen?** Allow for responses. Choose two students to read the story of the call of Jeremiah in Jeremiah 1:4-10. Let one student be Jeremiah and read his words, and the other be the voice of the Lord. If time allows, read it through several times, allowing different kids to participate. **According to these verses, how did Jeremiah feel about being chosen?** (Scared, inadequate, young and inexperienced.) **Do you think he wanted to be a prophet?** (Probably not.) **As a prophet, what would he be asked to do?** (Speak God's words to kings and rulers.) Explore with your class the fact that Jeremiah would have been well acquainted with God's prophets and what they did, and that the good ones were not popular! Often, prophets were chosen by God to tell kings and very powerful rulers that what they were doing was wrong and that God expected them to change their ways. Although many would respond

positively to this, others were angry (as we might expect!) and had God's prophets killed. Certainly, Jeremiah was thinking about what it would take to be this kind of person, and as we can see in verse six, he felt unqualified and too young.

Even though Jeremiah may have felt too young and not qualified, what was the one good reason why he could respond positively to God's invitation to him? Refer to verses seven and eight. (God had a plan for Jeremiah and promised to be with him every step of the way.) **Did you know that you are much like Jeremiah? God has a purpose for creating each one of you special and unique. He has a plan for you, and wants to see that His plan is fulfilled in you. Remember, no one can take your place! Only you can do that which God has planned for you to do. Doesn't that help you know how important you are? It helped Jeremiah to be able to follow God's plan for his life, even though he felt young and unqualified. He held on to God's hand and went on to be one of the greatest prophets that ever lived!**

Distribute copies of the activity sheet "You Can Bank On It!" (page 16). **Have you ever heard of the expression, "Save for a rainy day" or "You can take that to the bank!"? What do they mean?** (We all need to have things we can count on to help us in troubled times: money for emergencies, people we can count on to help, things we know are true to help us when we feel discouraged or as if we don't measure up.) Remind your class that Jeremiah knew what it was like to have doubts about himself, and that the job he was asked to do was just too big! During those times, he learned to take God's promises and deposit them into his memory bank. No doubt, those promises kept him going on more than one occasion.

Complete the first part of the activity sheet together, talking about each verse. Help the kids turn each statement into an "I" statement before writing them in the blanks. Possible responses: Jeremiah 1:5: I formed you in the womb. I knew you before you were born. I set you apart. Jeremiah 1:8: I am with you and will rescue you. Jeremiah 1:9: I have put my words in your mouth. Jeremiah 1:10: I appoint you over nations and kingdoms.

Now go on to the second part of the sheet, looking for God's words of help to us from each verse listed. Turn each of these into an "I" statement as well. Possible responses: Genesis 1:27: I created you in my image. Genesis 1:31: I looked at what I made (YOU) and saw it was good. Joshua 1:5: I will be with you. I will never leave you nor forsake you. Psalm 32:8: I will instruct you and teach you in the way you should go. I will counsel you and watch over you. Isaiah 41:10: I am with you. I am your God. I will strengthen you and help you with my right hand. Jeremiah 29:11: I know the plans I have for you; plans to

prosper you and not to harm you, plans to give you hope and a future. John 14:27: I give my peace to you.

God knew that at times, regardless of our age or circumstances, we would all struggle with who we are and how we feel about ourselves. He gave these assurances to us to help us like ourselves and be satisfied with the way He made us. What do you have to do before you can receive cash from a check? (Endorse or sign the back of it.) **When you sign the back of a check, you are telling the bank that you are receiving the money. Sign the deposit slips on the sheet so that you will be able to cash in on God's assurances someday when you need to remember His love and plan for you!**

Summarize this section by referring to the Unit Verse, Isaiah 43:4. Ask the kids to find it in their Bibles and read it aloud together. Perhaps this verse says it all! No matter what we may think of ourselves, this is God's opinion of us.

✔ Living the Lesson (5-10 minutes)

We've talked about how we are each created in a unique way and different from anyone else in the world. God values each one of us and loves the way He made us! But sometimes it's hard for us to see ourselves as special and unique. Sometimes it's easier for others to see how God has created us with special talents and abilities. Direct the kid's attention to the banner entitled "Thank You God for Me." Instruct them to glue or tape their fingerprint names to the banner. **Our fingerprints are just one indication of how different we really are. We have different names, talents, and abilities. We're going to end our class today by letting others know some of the things we like best about the way God has created them.** Allow time for class members to go to the banner and write one phrase on each of the fingerprint name sheets. Discuss some appropriate phrases to write for each other. Some possibilities are: You're a good friend, a good sport, outstanding team player, have beautiful eyes, make me laugh. Be sure the statements are true expressions of feelings about each other. See that each fingerprint paper has at least one phrase written on it.

End today's session with a group huddle prayer. Thank God for His perfect design for each one of us. Encourage the children to look for ways to show appreciation for all of God's creation this week.

Created Unique!

Cut apart these statements. Look up each verse and read each statement. Decide whether the information is true about only humans, only animals, or about both. Then place it in the bag with a label that matches your decision.

Can use a computer skillfully	Can read a book of the Bible
Has favorite foods	Learn behaviors from their parents
Genesis 1:27	Can live underwater without life support
Genesis 1:25	Come in a wide variety of shapes, sizes, and colors
Matthew 6:26	Can have a personal relationship with God
Some are becoming extinct	John 3:16
Have distinct personalities	Were made by God to be ruled by man

- - - - - - - - - - - - **cut here** - - - - - - - - - - - - -

PLAY DETECTIVE!

Listed below are three of the four major fingerprint classifications. The fourth category is named "Accidental" and has no pattern at all. Which one looks most like your fingerprints?

ARCH

LOOP

WHORL

 # "You Can Bank on It!"

Look up each Scripture reference in your Bible. Decide what assurance or guarantee God is making to Jeremiah. Try to start all your phrases with the word "I", as if God were speaking.

1ST BANK OF GOD'S ASSURANCE, ANYTOWN, USA 12230-2222

FOR DEPOSIT ONLY!   Account #123-456-789

   Deposit to the account of: JEREMIAH, GOD'S PROPHET

Jeremiah 1:5 _____

Jeremiah 1:8 _____

Jeremiah 1:9 _____

Jeremiah 1:10 _____

⑈122007⑊94⑈   ***National Bank of Judah***

Now look up these verses and decide what guarantee God is making to YOU! Then deposit this list of God's assurances in your memory bank to remind yourself how much He loves you and cares about you.

1ST BANK OF GOD'S ASSURANCE, ANYTOWN, USA 12230-2222

FOR DEPOSIT ONLY!   Account # _____

Deposit to the account of:_____
                                                      (write your name here)

Genesis 1:27 _____

Genesis 1:31 _____

Joshua 1:5 _____

Psalm 32:8 _____

Isaiah 41:10 _____

Jeremiah 29:11 _____

John 14:27 _____

THESE ASSURANCES WERE RECEIVED BY: _____
                                                         (sign your name here)

⑈6420190⑊12⑈   (write today's date here) _____

I Approve!

Aim: That your students will accept themselves the way God created them and not compare themselves to others.

Scripture: Judges 6:1-16
Unit Verse: You are precious and honored in my sight, and . . . I love you. Isaiah 43:4
Unit Affirmation: I CAN LIKE MYSELF!

✓ Planning Ahead

1. Photocopy Activity Sheets (pages 23 and 24)—one for each student.
2. Prepare the Consumer Comparison Stations as described in SETTING THE STAGE.
4. Have available at least one of the following: binoculars, a kaleidoscope, several pieces of different colored cellophane (about 4" x 6" each).

 Setting the Stage (5-10 minutes)
WHAT YOU'LL DO
• Conduct three Consumer Comparisons
WHAT YOU'LL NEED
• Items for Consumer Comparison Stations

 Introducing the Issue (20 minutes)
WHAT YOU'LL DO
• Explore comparisons and the problems they can cause
• Use an activity sheet to help identify ways and places we compare ourselves with others
• Add a phrase to the Unit Affirmation poster
WHAT YOU'LL NEED
• One apple and one orange
• "The Comparison Trap" Activity Sheet (page 23)
• Unit Affirmation poster

 Searching the Scriptures (20 minutes)
WHAT YOU'LL DO
• Research Gideon's feelings of inadequacy when he compared himself with others
• Document how God used Gideon to accomplish a spectacular victory
WHAT YOU'LL NEED
• Chalkboard or poster

4 **Living the Lesson** (5-10 minutes)
WHAT YOU'LL DO
• Recognize that our perception does not change the way things are
• Use an activity sheet to list some personal valuable qualities
• Thank God for making us unique and different
WHAT YOU'LL NEED
• Pair of binoculars, a kaleidoscope, and/or several pieces of different colored cellophane
• "God's Plan: Nothing Can Compare!" Activity Sheet (page 24)

 Setting the Stage (5-10 minutes)

Before your students arrive today, set up three activity stations around the room:

1. SOFT DRINK TASTE TEST. Pour small cups of Coke and Pepsi. Put all of one brand on the left side of the table, the other on the right. Have some soda cracker pieces available on a napkin. Make a tally sheet for each one to mark a preference. Have the children taste and compare the two drinks and decide which they like best. Print these instructions on a card and place at this station:

1. Taste a drink from the right side of the table.
2. Eat a cracker.
3. Taste a drink from the left side of the table.
4. Decide which drink you like better. Record your preference on the tally sheet by putting a check mark under Left or Right.

2. PAPER TOWEL ABSORBENCY TEST. Provide two different brands of paper towels. Take off the labels and mark them Roll #1 and Roll #2. Make a tally sheet for each one to mark a preference. Place the towels and a small bowl of water on the table. Print these instructions on a card and place at this station:

1. Tear off one towel from each roll.
2. Dip each towel into the water.
3. Decide which one is most absorbent. Record your preference on the tally sheet by putting a check mark under #1 or #2.

3. INGREDIENT COMPARISON. Display three different brands of cereal, each wrapped in a brown paper bag with only the ingredient list and nutrition information exposed. Label boxes #1, #2, and #3. Pour a small amount of cereal in very small cups and place these in front of the boxes for tasting. Make a tally sheet for each one to mark a preference. Print these instructions on a card and place at this station:

1. Read the ingredient list and nutritional information on each box.
2. Taste each cereal.
3. Decide which cereal is the best tasting and which one is the healthiest to eat.
4. Record the number of your choice on the tally sheet under the correct column: #1, #2, or #3—Good For You or Tastes Good.

As kids arrive, instruct them to visit one of the three stations. When all have had a chance to compare at least one set of products, gather everyone together. Review the findings and reveal winners for each test. **Did everyone agree on which was best? Why or why not?** (We all have different standards and tastes.) **How did you make your decision? What would happen if we only had one of each**

kind of product and there were no choices? (We would have to settle for what we had!) **Whether it's soft drinks, paper towels, or cereal, differences make our world a better and more interesting place to live. Differences among people also make our lives richer and more interesting. But those differences often lead us to make comparisons among ourselves and others. Sometimes that can be good, but more often comparing ourselves to others leaves us feeling scared and feeling inadequate. Let's take a closer look at what happens when we compare ourselves with others.**

✓ Introducing the Issue (20 minutes)

Can you think of a time when you compared yourself to someone else? How did it make you feel? (Sometimes better, sometimes worse!) **Why do you think we compare ourselves with others?** (To make ourselves feel better or because we wish we were more like them, because we feel inferior and critical of ourselves.) Hold up an apple and an orange. **Have you ever heard the expression, "It's like comparing apples and oranges"? Apples and oranges are the same, yet different. How are they the same?** (Round, fruit, juicy, nutritious.) **But if you've ever tasted the two, you know that they are also very different. Name some ways they are different.** (Appearance, taste, color.) **Yet God created the apple to be an apple, not an orange. And He created the orange to be an orange, not an apple. We don't have orange apples or red oranges do we?**

Now supposing the apple looked at the orange one day and said, "Wow, I think being orange is the coolest! I hate being red! I just know I'd be so much happier being orange!" What if it even pretended to be an orange? Would that make it an orange? Explain that comparing itself with another piece of fruit will not change the apple. It was designed to be an apple and that's the what it will always be. God made it to be an apple. The plans were in the seed that created it. **In the same way God made you to be you! Not someone else! He had a special plan in mind when He made each one of us, and that plan is designed to prepare us to bring glory to Him in our own special and original way. Unfortunately, many times we get caught acting more like the apple wanting to be an orange. In fact, we all get caught in this "Comparison Trap"!**

Distribute copies of the activity sheet "The Comparison Trap" (page 23). Divide the kids into groups of three or four and instruct them to use five minutes to think of as many answers as possible for each category. The group

with the most answers at the end of five minutes will win. Possible answers include:

WHAT: appearance, size, shape, color, clothes, grades.
WHERE: school, home, church, Little League, Sunday school.
HOW: putting ourselves down, wishing we looked like them.
WHO: friends, family, baseball stars, movie stars, pastors, teachers.

Briefly review and discuss their lists together as a group. **Maybe you've heard the phrase "God doesn't make junk." That statement is 100% true. He has made each one of us in His image and with a specific purpose in mind. We need to remember that fact when we are tempted to wish we were more like someone else!**

Display the Unit Affirmation poster where all can see it. Read it aloud together. Let kids suggest phrases and add one. Some suggestions are: by feeling satisfied with who I am and how God made me, by realizing God doesn't make junk, by being happy with the way God made me.

The Bible is full of examples of God using people who felt unqualified and scared to do the things God asked them to do. Let's take a look at a man who felt as if he didn't measure up to others and see how God used him in a mighty way!

Searching the Scriptures (20 minutes)

Review with the class that last week they talked about Jeremiah. When God told Jeremiah that he would be a famous prophet and would guide and direct the entire nation of Judah, he felt inadequate and frightened. **This week's Bible person and Jeremiah had a lot in common. Let's see how much!** Have kids find Judges 6:12 in their Bibles and discover who this week's Bible person is (Gideon). Fill them in on some of this background information found in Judges 6:1-10.

The nation of Israel had not obeyed God again! God had delivered them from Pharaoh's hands in Egypt, but they had since gone back to some of their old habits and fallen prey to another nation—the Midianites. The Midianites had invaded Israel's land, stolen their crops, and ravaged their land. The Israelites were forced into the mountains to live in caves. They feared for their lives and cried out to the Lord for help! In answer, God sent an angel to recruit a leader to defend the Israelites and recapture their land.

Have a volunteer read Judges 6:11, 12. **What was Gideon doing when the angel appeared to him?** (Threshing wheat in a winepress to keep it from the Midianites.) **Basically he was hiding grain from the enemy. It was very hard**

work. He was probably sweaty, tired, and frustrated. This was work often done by servants. How did the angel greet Gideon? (The Lord is with you, mighty warrior.) **Do you think Gideon felt either statement was true?** (Probably not!) His people were in hiding, they had been robbed, killed. and chased from their land. It certainly didn't feel like God was with him! And how about that mighty warrior phrase? Did a mighty warrior thresh wheat in a winepress? This was considered to be a servant's hot, sweaty, and boring job! Gideon expressed these feelings in verse 13. Choose a child to read verses 13, 14. **What is the angel telling Gideon here?** (That God had answered the Israelites' prayers to be rescued from the hands of the Midianites and Gideon was God's man for the job!)

Let's zero in on verse 15 to see Gideon's response to God's request. Read the verse aloud with lots of expression, and then ask the class to paraphrase Gideon's response. Some examples might be: Who me? Are You nuts, God? I'm no warrior! You've got the wrong man! I come from a nothing family and I'm the biggest nothing in it!

Gideon definitely did not agree with God's assessment of the best man for the job. Just like Jeremiah, he did not see himself through God's eyes. He felt unqualified and unprepared for the job. God answered Gideon's questions in verse 16 when He guaranteed His presence and the success of the battle. If we follow this story through to the end, we see that not only does God help Gideon defeat the Midianites, but He does so in a clever way! Who can re-member how the story ends? (Gideon recruits troops to help him, but God keeps eliminating them until there are only 300. With clay pots and torches, they scare the Midianites into fleeing the land.)

If Gideon had seen himself from God's perspective, do you think he would have been more confident about accepting the job God had for him? Allow time for response. Make a list of the qualities God must have seen, even though Gideon obviously did not see them in himself. List together the strengths God found in Gideon that allowed him to serve the Lord as the leader of the battle. Some suggestions are: obedience, creativity, strength, discernment, leadership, intelligence, courage.

Just like Gideon, we can be confident that God made us exactly the way we need to be to serve Him. We can get this confidence by learning to look at ourselves from God's perspective instead of comparing ourselves to others.

OPTIONAL: Let's join Gideon's army for a few minutes and affirm the fact that we are God's special creation. Use the following words to the army cadence, "Sound Off" for a march. If you have the space available, line up the kids and march around the room as they repeat the following phrases after you:

> God designed me like I am (Repeat)
> He made me with His own hands (Repeat)
> Special plans He has for me (Repeat)
> Thank You God that I am me! (Repeat)
> Thank You (Repeat)
> Thank You (Repeat)
> Thank You God, for me! (Repeat)

Gather everyone together in a circle for a prayer huddle. Go around the circle, with the students completing this sentence naming one characteristic about themselves which they value: "Thank You, God, for making me . . . ."

✓ Living the Lesson (5-10 minutes)

Place the following objects in the center of your table: a pair of binoculars, a kaleidoscope, several pieces of colored cellophane. Choose something in the room to focus on, such as a picture or a window. Allow a few minutes for your students to look at the focus point through each of the objects (including both ends of the binoculars). **How did the _____ (name the focus point) look through the different things you looked through?** Allow for responses. **Did the _____ actually change just because we looked at it through a pair of binoculars?** (No. What is real does not change, only our perception of it.) **We have to be very careful when we look at, and form opinions about ourselves. Comparing ourselves to others can be like seeing ourselves through the wrong end of a binoculars, or through colored cellophane, and we will probably end up believing something about ourselves that isn't real!**

Distribute copies of the activity sheet "God's Plan: Nothing Can Compare" (page 24) and read the Unit Verse together. **The only way we can be sure we are seeing what is real about ourselves is to see ourselves through the perspective of God's Word. Our Unit Verse, which we just read, is a terrific verse to take out and read on days when we feel down about who we are and what we can do.** Have kids write some things they like about the way God has made them. Be prepared to make suggestions or give encouragement to those who have a hard time seeing anything good about themselves. Outside traits might include: beautiful hair, eyes, hands, strong muscles, healthy legs, nice teeth. Inside qualities might include: intelligent, responsible, loving, energetic, sensitive to others. As they leave today, encourage them to tuck this list into their Bibles where it can be added to and serve as a reminder of how God created them as unique and gifted individuals!

The Comparison Trap ✓

WHAT: THINGS WE COMPARE ABOUT OURSELVES	WHERE: PLACES WE COMPARE OURSELVES

HOW: WAYS WE COMPARE OURSELVES	**WHO: PEOPLE WITH WHOM WE COMPARE OURSELVES**

God's Plan: Nothing Can Compare!

Thanks, God, for making me! Here's a list of the things I like best about me!

My outside:

1._____
2._____
3._____

My inside:

1._____
2._____
3._____

You are precious and
honored in my sight,
and . . . I love you.
Isaiah 43:4

Lesson 3

Sticks and Stones . . .

Aim: That your students will avoid letting the opinions of others affect how they feel about themselves.
Scripture: Genesis 6:5-15, 22
Unit Verse: You are precious and honored in my sight, and . . . I love you. Isaiah 43:4
Unit Affirmation: I CAN LIKE MYSELF!

 Planning Ahead

1. Photocopy Activity Sheets (pages 31 and 32)—one for each student.
2. Prepare two Graffiti Walls. Cut two 6' - 8' foot pieces of shelf or computer paper. Write this title on one paper: STICKS AND STONES. Title the other paper: THE POWER OF WORDS . . . TO HELP! Attach these Graffiti Walls to different walls in the room at a height appropriate for your students to write on.
3. Make 55 letter cards for a Reaction Game. Write one letter on each 4" x 6" card for each of these phrases. "Share Your Feelings" "Repay evil with good" "Believe only what is true." Attach the cards to the wall so the letters can't be seen (facing the wall) and so each phrase can be read when the letters are all turned around. Attach the letter cards that complete each separate phrase to different areas in the room.

 1 Setting the Stage (5-10 minutes)
WHAT YOU'LL DO
- Write words and phrases on a Graffiti Wall as examples of how people's comments can hurt us
WHAT YOU'LL NEED
- STICKS AND STONES Graffiti Wall

 2 Introducing the Issue (20 minutes)
WHAT YOU'LL DO
- Discuss how we are affected by things others say
- Play the Reaction Game to discover ways to handle hurtful comments
- Use an activity sheet to practice dealing with hurtful situations
- Add a phrase to the Unit Affirmation poster
WHAT YOU'LL NEED
- STICKS AND STONES Graffiti Wall
- Letter cards
- "And Then What Happened?" Activity Sheet (Page 31)
- Unit Affirmation poster

3 Searching the Scriptures (20 minutes)
WHAT YOU'LL DO
- Dramatize a story to discover how Noah did not allow the opinions of others to interfere with his obedience to God
- List words that describe God's unchanging opinion of us
- **OPTIONAL:** Measure an area to visualize the enormity of Noah's project and his potential embarrassment
WHAT YOU'LL NEED
- "Noah Navigates Through Nitpickers" Activity Sheet (Page 32)

 4 Living the Lesson (5-10 minutes)
WHAT YOU'LL DO
- Write encouraging messages and words on a Graffiti Wall
WHAT YOU'LL NEED
- THE POWER OF WORDS. . .TO HELP Graffiti Wall

Setting the Stage (5-10 minutes)

As your students arrive today, direct them to the STICKS AND STONES Graffiti Wall as a way to begin thinking about the power words can have. They are to write on it words or phrases that are negative and hurtful, such as put–downs they may have experienced, both as the sender and the receiver. If necessary, set some limits for this activity: no profanity or unacceptable words. Some suggestions are: geek, nerd, fatso, goody-two-shoes, flubberbuster, dumbo, stupid, ugly, dingbat, That's an ugly shirt!, You ride that old bike?, You live in a dump!, What did you expect from Miss Perfect?

NOTE: You will need to be especially sensitive to your class today. Some of the words they will hear and the experiences they share later may still be hurtful and fresh in their minds. We're asking them to be vulnerable by sharing past hurts. Set some ground rules for your discussions: no put–downs, respect everyone's feelings, what is said in this class session stays in this room!

After a few minutes, gather the children together to talk about the phrases and the feelings the words evoke. **Have you ever heard the phrase "Sticks and Stones may break my bones, but words can never hurt me"? Is that statement true?** (No.) **Why or why not?** (Words can hurt us deeply, words might hurt more than physical attacks.)
When we are hurt physically because of wounds from sticks and stones it's easy to see the injury. But when we are hurt by words, the wounds are deep inside us where nobody can see. Sometimes the inside hurts cause more pain than a skinned knee or cut! The words we use have great power to cause deep feelings. Can any of you think of a time when someone's words hurt you deep inside? Allow time for responses. Have an experience from your own life to share with the class so they understand that you too have shared their experiences.

Introducing the Issue (20 minutes)

We naturally care what other people think about us. We want others to like us and think we are valuable, intelligent, and acceptable. When they don't, it can feel uncomfortable and hurt! God understands the feelings we have when others hurt us with words. He even thought those feeling were important enough to talk about in the Bible. Let's look at a verse that shows how God understands the way words can

hurt. Ask a volunteer to read Proverbs 18:8.

Let's look at the phrase "down to a man's inmost parts." What do you think that means? (Inside yourself, your feelings, thoughts, and pride.) **Think of a time when several of your friends put you down or made fun of you. Why would gossip be compared to a choice morsel?** (Sometimes others enjoy getting together and talking about someone else in a negative way. They enjoy picking on people.)

Your class will probably agree that the words people say to us have tremendous power, both negative and positive! They can make us feel really, really good about ourselves (You're the Best!), or really, really bad about ourselves (You clumsy nerd—you dropped the ball again!) Point out to your students that we can't always control what other people say to us, but we can control how we choose to respond to what they say. Whether we realize it or not, we do decide how we will react. Most of the time, the words that hurt us are not even true, but are said out of anger or insensitivity and should never have been said in the first place. At those times, it is important to make a big effort to reject those harsh words and not let them get through to us.

Standing our ground when people make fun or knowing how to respond to hurtful comments is not easy—no matter how old we get. It can help to think about how to react and come up with some options before we find ourselves in the middle of the situation. Let's look at some ways we can handle these put-downs and opinions when they're directed at us. Using the letter cards attached to the wall, play the Reaction game. Start with one phrase, divide the class into two teams and let them take turns guessing letters. Write down each letter guessed so they won't guess the same letter twice. When they guess a correct letter, turn it over. Allow them to guess until they know the phrase. As they guess the phrases, ask the following questions: **Have you ever used this response or reaction? Did it work? What was the outcome? What are the risks? Which do you use the most often? Are all these responses ones God would honor and like?**

PHRASES:
Share your feelings
Repay evil with good
Believe only what is true

Now that you know a few ways to handle put–downs, let's look at some actual situations where you might have to use some of these techniques. Distribute copies of the activity sheet "And Then What Happened?" (page 31). **We've all run into situations where we have to choose how to handle someone's negative comment. Read through the cartoon strip and decide on two different ways this scene could end. Draw your conclusion in the boxes below.** Divide the class into pairs and allow time for them to complete their drawings. Then ask a few to share their solutions with the rest of the class.

> **OPTIONAL:** If you have a longer class time, let the kids prepare their scenarios as skits and present them to the rest of the class.

Display the Unit Affirmation poster and ask the class to read the Affirmation aloud. Review each of the phrases listed so far. **What phrase can we add to show how we can like ourselves in spite of others' opinions?** Let the class think of phrases to add today. Possibilities include, "by letting God's opinion matter most," or "by asking God to help me tune out others' negative opinions." Agree on one and add it to the third line. **Now let's go to our Bibles and take a look at a man who had a lot of experience tuning out what others said!**

 # Searching the Scriptures (20 minutes)

Have the kids find Genesis 6:8 in their Bibles, and discover who today's lesson is about. **You may be familiar with the story of Noah. Today we want to look at a part of the story you may not have noticed before.** Choose a volunteer to read Genesis 6:7-15 aloud. **How does God describe Noah in these verses?** (Found favor in the eyes of the Lord; righteous, blameless, walked with God.) **How are the earth and its people described?** (Corrupt in God's sight, full of violence.) **What do you think that means?** Let the kids respond. Point out that people in Noah's day were not unlike people in our own day. Many had abandoned any belief or commitment to God, and followed their own natural instincts in their actions. No doubt Noah's contemporaries were into abuse, neglect, murders, rape, and other violent crimes. **Imagine how bad things must have been for God to come to Noah and say that He was sorry He had created people in the first place, and that He was now going to destroy everyone He had created! Except for one very special man, who continued to believe and trust in God no matter what happened around him. And trusting God became really difficult as God came to him and made an incredible request!**

> **OPTIONAL:** If time allows, you might consider impressing the kids with just how large a task this was for Noah. The Bible tells us that the ark was 450 feet long, 75 feet wide and 45 feet high. That is the distance of 1-1/2 football fields and three stories high. To help the kids visualize this, find an area outside that is 450 feet long and take the kids out to walk this distance. You might want to locate a spot where you could sit and finish the lesson outside. Or you could walk the halls of your church, or estimate how many times you would have to

walk around the inside of your classroom to make 450 feet. Make a visual, concrete impression on the kids about the extent of this project for Noah, and how foolish he must have looked to his contemporaries watching him build a gigantic boat in the middle of the desert!

Noah had a tough job! To make an ark to the specifications God gave was an awesome undertaking. He didn't have power tools like circular saws or electric drills. He didn't have much help either. The only help he probably received was from his three sons and their families. But the physical labor was only a part of what made his job so difficult! There was also a lot of emotional stress.

Distribute copies of the activity sheet "Noah Navigates Through Nitpickers" (page 32). Be sure your kids understand what a nitpicker is: someone who always finds something wrong with the details of things, and is always on hand with something negative to say. Choose several volunteers to play the main parts, and then instruct the rest of the class that they will also participate as the crowd. Set the scene by telling everyone that they are the residents of Noah's town, and they have all come out to see what this weird guy is doing—building an incredibly huge boat! Then let the kids present the skit.

OPTIONAL: If your class is large and you have time, create several groups and have them rehearse the skit at this time. Then arrange for them to present their skits to other classes.

None of us escapes criticism and harassment from others. Noah was no exception. Which do you think was harder: physically building the ark or putting up with all the harassment and comments of people around him? Why? Allow for responses.

We talked last week about looking at ourselves from God's perspective and not the world's. The opinions of those around us can change minute by minute. Name some things that shape other's opinions of us. (Their mood, actions, circumstances, and past experiences.) All of these things are changeable. Sometimes people are in good moods. Other times they're in terrible moods. Some people are angry and want to hurt others. **People's opinions change on a daily basis. Sometimes minute by minute. And people's opinions are very often different from God's. Noah found favor in God's eyes but not in the eyes of the people around him. The good news is that God's opinion of us never changes. Our Unit Verse declares God's opinion of us: We are precious and honored in His sight. Nothing we can ever do or say can change God's opinion of us. We need to know that when others make us feel inferior or stupid, God is there to remind us that we are precious and honored!**

To help the kids understand this verse better, ask the class to think of other words (synonyms) for the key words in the verse. Ask them to suggest synonyms for "precious" and "honored." Write their answers on a chalkboard or poster board. Examples for precious: loved, valued, priceless, rare, cherished, beloved, worth a lot, dear. Examples for honored: publicly recognized, accepted, admired, respected. **It would be nice if we could call God on the phone and hear Him tell us how He feels about us. Unfortunately that's not an option. But we can turn to His Word for this information. The Unit Verse is a great reminder of how God loves us and feels about us. Let's use this verse as a way of keeping our perspective. When others hurt our feelings or put us down, we will remember God's opinion!**

✓ Living the Lesson (5-10 minutes)

We have seen how words can be hurtful. But words can also be very positive and healing in our lives. Refer to the Graffiti Wall STICKS AND STONES, and then to the second Graffiti Wall labeled THE POWER OF WORDS . . . TO HELP. Refer back to the list of synonyms written on the board. **Which of these words would you like to hear God speak to you?** Let them choose a favorite synonym and write it on the Graffiti Wall. Now fill up the wall with other words that are powerful in a helpful way. Suggest that words be written that are the opposite in meaning to those on the STICKS AND STONES Graffiti Wall. Consider expressions that will build up another person instead of hurting. Possibilities are: I'm glad you're my friend, You did a great job!, You have the best smile in the whole world.

End with a prayer of thanksgiving to God for His acceptance and love for each of us.

And Then What Happened?

Directions: In the boxes below, draw two DIFFERENT responses Laura could have made to her friends.

. . . AND THEN WHAT HAPPENED?

Noah Navigates Through Nitpickers

CHARACTERS: Announcer, Noah, Abner, Gladys, Japheth, God, Crowd

ANNOUNCER: Good morning ladies and gentlemen. Today we're going to look in on some very famous Bible characters: Noah and his family. We've caught Noah in the middle of a typical day. He's working on the ark that God told him to build. Let's see what kind of day he's having. SHHH . . . listen!

NOAH (Confused): Let's see, where was that tape measure. I need to check these measurements again. Ah, there it is.

ABNER: See Gladys, I told you he was building something. What it is I can't imagine, but it sure is big.

GLADYS: It sure is! It's going to ruin property value! Who will want to live beside this thing! What is it anyway?

NOAH (to himself): Let's see, God said it should be 450 feet long, 75 feet wide and 45 feet high. Whew, that sure is huge! God, are You sure it has to be that big?

GOD: Yes, Noah, that's exactly right. Trust Me, I know what I'm doing.

NOAH: O.K. God, but this is really really big! Our front yard is becoming a tourist attraction.

ABNER: He told me it was an ARK.

GLADYS: An ark? What is an ark?

ABNER: Some kind of boat or ship. But we're miles from water. I think he's lost his marbles! Maybe we should get some neighbors together and picket his house.

JAPHETH: Dad, have you seen all those people out front? They're carrying signs and yelling rude remarks. They're such nitpickers. They all have some nasty comment to make! One sign says "Noah's a Nutcake," another says "Neighbors Against Noah." This is so embarrassing. Do you have to build this thing?

NOAH: Japheth, God gave me specific instructions and I've got to obey them. I know this isn't easy, how do you think I feel? Yesterday when I was coating a section with pitch, people started throwing tomatoes at me. But this is what God has told me. I must trust Him and do what's right. Are you with me?

JAPHETH: Yeah, I guess so. But it's really hard when all of them think we're nuts.

NOAH: I know, but God doesn't think we're nuts. He cared about our family enough to trust us with this job. He has promised to protect us and we've got to keep our end of the bargain. Come on, help me with this board.

CROWD CHANTING TOGETHER: Noah's a nutcake! Noah's a nutcake! Move that thing somewhere else! Who do you think you are? You gonna carry it to the beach? It'll never float!

GOD: Noah, it's pretty rough down there, isn't it?

NOAH (Hesitantly): Well, ah, yes Lord.

GOD: Noah, the opinion of those other people doesn't really matter. You have found favor in My eyes! You are a righteous, blameless man among the people of your time. You have walked with Me and remained loyal to Me. I want you to know I love you! You are precious in My sight.

NOAH: Thanks God! I really needed to hear that right now.

GOD: Just remember that what I think about you is what counts, Noah. Wait until the rain starts to fall! Then we'll see what their opinion is of you!

Lesson 4

Talking to Myself

Aim: That your students will avoid thinking and talking negatively about themselves but instead, with God's help, build themselves up in positive ways.

Scripture: I Timothy 4:12-16a

Unit Verse: You are precious and honored in my sight, and . . . I love you. Isaiah 43:4

Unit Affirmation: I CAN LIKE MYSELF!

 Planning Ahead

1. Photocopy Activity Sheets (pages 39 and 40)—one for each student.
2. Record cassettes and write instructions as described in SETTING THE STAGE.
3. Collect the following items: sieve with very small holes (such as a tea strainer), one to two teaspoons of sugar or salt, a cup of water, small bowl or other container.
4. Write the following Scripture references and notes on five separate pieces of paper. Fold the papers and put them in a container so they can be taken out anonymously. PSALM 139:13-14, ZEPHANIAH 3:17, EPHESIANS 1:4—change the word "us" to "me", JOHN 3:16—change "the world" to "me", PHILIPPIANS 1:6—change "you" to "me."

1 Setting the Stage (5-10 minutes)

WHAT YOU'LL DO

- Participate in a listening and remembering activity

WHAT YOU'LL NEED

- Four cassette tape recorders
- Four pre-recorded cassettes

2 Introducing the Issue (20 minutes)

WHAT YOU'LL DO

- Illustrate how our brains may filter out messages
- Use an activity sheet to translate negative messages into positive ones.
- Add a phrase to the Unit Affirmation poster

WHAT YOU'LL NEED

- Demonstration items
- "Strain that Brain!" Activity Sheet (page 39)
- Unit Affirmation poster

3 Searching the Scriptures (20 minutes)

WHAT YOU'LL DO

- Use an activity sheet to observe ways a mature Christian friend helped a young man

WHAT YOU'LL NEED

- "Three Cheers for Timothy!" Activity Sheet (page 40)
- **OPTIONAL:** *The Little Engine That Could* by Watty Piper

4 Living the Lesson (5-10 minutes)

WHAT YOU'LL DO

- Design a cheer from a Bible verse about God's attitude

WHAT YOU'LL NEED

- Scripture references in a container

Lesson 4

✓ Setting the Stage (5-10 minutes)

Before class, record a group of ten statements three times on each cassette to be used. Read the list through once, pausing between each statement, and then read the entire list again two more times so the groups will not need to rewind the tape. Begin the statements with the words "You" and "I". Such as:

- You dropped the ball. I'm a klutz!
- You broke the vase, stupid. I can't do anything right!
- You look great today. I look great today.
- You got a D on your report. I'm really stupid.
- You played a great game! I'm a good player.

Write the following instructions on a chalkboard or poster board so they can be read by the students as they arrive: Go to a listening station and turn on the cassette recorder. Listen very carefully to the statements on the tape. There are ten messages on the tape and they will be repeated three times. Try to remember as many of the statements as possible. When the tape is finished, turn it off and write down as many statements as you remember.

Set up four stations with a cassette recorder and writing paper at each station.

To begin today's session, your students will listen to a cassette tape recorded with several statements. After everyone has arrived and had a chance to participate in the activity, gather the group together. **Your brain received many messages on that tape. Some were easier to remember than others. Which statements were easiest for you to remember?** Make a list of the statements they remembered on a board or paper. **Were the positive statements** (looking great, good player) **easier to remember than the putdowns? Why do you think some were easier to remember than others? Today we are going to talk about the messages your brain sends and receives, and how they can affect the way you feel about yourself.**

✓ Introducing the Issue (20 minutes)

The messages you heard were the kind that come from two different sources. What were they? (Outside — someone saying something to us, and inside — something I say to myself.) **Some were examples of people talking to us and others were examples of the way we talk to ourselves. When the first person said, "You dropped the ball," the inside response might be, "I'm a bad player." Is that statement necessarily true?** (No!)

Lesson 4

Why or why not? (The ball could have taken a bad bounce. The sun could have been in your eyes. Your could have made one mistake out of 25 games! You might be having an off day.)

We receive millions of messages everyday. Some messages are from things other people say to us, and some are things we say to ourselves. Some are positive messages and some are negative. What do we mean by the words, "negative" and "positive"? When we give ourselves messages about ourselves, we are engaging in something we call "self-talk." Messages such as, "I'm really good at this," or "I'm such a nerd", are both examples of self- talk, and both messages affect the way we think and feel about ourselves.

Let's look at an example of what happens when our brains receive messages about ourselves from others around us. Display the sieve and other items in PLANNING AHEAD. **We receive thousands of messages everyday. Where do these messages come from?** (TV, teachers, parents, friends, coaches.) **Are all of the messages we hear true?** (No!) Explain that because not everything we hear is true, our brain must listen to each message and sort out what to believe and what to reject; what's true and what's not. **Just like this sieve, it must allow some information to pass through and strain other messages out. Someone may say 2 + 2 = 4. Your brain hears that and knows from past experience that it is 100% true. That information flows right through. If I poured this water through the sieve, what would happen?** (It would go right on through without affecting it very much—just get it wet.) **But then a friend might say "You turkey! What did you do that for?"** Pour some sugar or salt in the sieve without allowing it to fall through the holes. **Your brain receives that message and you must make a decision. Will you believe the statement and think, "I am a turkey!" or "I can't do anything right!"?** Shake the sieve so that some of the sugar or salt comes through. **Or, will you strain out those messages as being untrue? "I'm not a turkey, I just made a mistake."** Pour all the sugar or salt out of the sieve. **There is a big difference between those two statements! Can you tell what it is?** Let kids respond. Make sure they understand that the first is an untrue statement that is self-destructive. The second is an accurate, true description of what happened. **Keeping these messages straight in our heads can be very tricky! The key to remember is this: negative self-talk is telling myself that I am no-good, bad, or stupid. Positive self-talk helps me think about what is really true and how I can grow. What are some examples of the two different kinds of statements?** Negative Self-Talk: I'm a klutz. I never do anything right. It's all my fault. As the kids name a put-down, throw some more items into the sieve. Positive Self-

Talk: I made a mistake. Playing baseball is not one of my strengths. I was mean to Joey; I will apologize. I'm a good friend.

It takes practice and help to learn to filter good information out from bad, or to turn a negative comment into a positive one. All the messages we hear about ourselves do affect us in some way. When it is difficult to filter out the hurting comments, ask God to help you do it. He can help you with things when you can't help yourself.

Distribute copies of the activity sheet "Strain that Brain!" (page 39). Go over the first example on the sheet together. Then write the statement, "I'm a crummy basketball player" on the board. Ask the kids to think of some additional statements that could replace that sentence and send a more positive message. Examples might be: I need to practice shooting baskets. I'm better at other sports than basketball. I had an off day playing today. **What would happen if every time I got ready to play basketball I thought to myself, "I'm a bad player. I won't make any baskets today. I'll probably embarrass myself and everyone will make fun of me."?** (We eventually act out what we believe to be true about ourselves; we will most likely play badly.) Have kids work in pairs to complete the other scenarios on their sheets. When completed, share responses.

Display the Unit Affirmation poster and review it together. Add a phrase such as, "by believing only what is true about me," or "by asking God to help me reject negative self-talk." Write the phrase on the fourth line. **Learning to accept what is true about ourselves and rejecting what is hurtful or untrue is hard work! It helps to spend time with people who are encouragers and help us affirm the good things about us. Now let's look at someone in the Bible who needed, and got, some encouragement from a special friend.**

✓ Searching the Scriptures (20 minutes)

Think back to a story you probably heard when you were little, about a train that was scared to go over a big hill. What was the message it repeated over and over to itself? (I think I can!)

> **OPTIONAL:** Locate a copy of the classic children's book *The Little Engine That Could* by Watty Piper and read it to your class. It is a powerful, yet simple illustration of today's lesson theme.

By repeating that message over and over and encouraging itself, the little

Lesson 4

train was able to chug right up the big hill. That's one illustration of how we can receive help from self-talk.

Another way to think of it is in terms of a cheering section at a game. **Have you ever been to a football game and listened to some of the cheers?** Give the kids an opportunity to share some of the popular cheers they've heard. **Cheers do many things for a team. Have you ever heard the cheer "You can do it, you can do it, you can, you can?" It's designed to encourage a team and "cheer them on" when the situation seems overwhelming. It helps them see their potential and abilities and work hard to win! Other cheers are designed to spur others on even though they are doing well. What are some that do this?** (We're #1. Who's the hardest team to beat? Go . . . name of team) **Still others give instructions on the best way to get the job done.** ("First and ten let's do it again! We like it! We like it!", is designed to tell the team to forge ahead and make another first down.) **Can you name some other cheers designed to tell the team what to do?** (Push them back. S.C.O.R.E. Score! Score!) All these cheers are good examples of giving positive messages to someone else. The team's job is to receive the messages and use them as energy to keep going!

Just like a team, people need encouragement, too. Our ability to receive and believe positive messages about ourselves is helped by people in our lives who will "cheer us on" by: 1) encouraging us when the going is rough, 2) spur us on to do even better when things are going well, and 3) give us helpful instructions about how to get a job done. Today's Bible lesson illustrates this process in action. Let's look at Timothy, who was going through a hard time and giving himself some negative self-talk because of it. His friend Paul took the time to send messages of encouragement!

Share some of the following background information with your class. First and II Timothy are both personal letters from Paul to Timothy. Timothy was serving as a pastor or overseer of the church at Ephesus, and Paul was in prison. Second Timothy is the last known letter of Paul before he was executed in Rome.

Paul and Timothy were very close friends. They had traveled together and spent a great deal of time working to spread the Good News of Jesus. Things Paul wrote show that Timothy may have been naturally shy and timid. But in spite of it, Timothy was so dependable and hard working that Paul bragged about him to others. Paul even refers to Timothy as "my true son in the faith" (I Timothy 1:2) and speaks highly of him to the Philippians (Philippians 2:19-22).

Timothy was facing a very difficult task. We know that he was young and working as an important leader in the church at Ephesus. We know from the Bible that this church had many problems. There was a lot of arguing and fighting going on within the church, and Paul was trusting Timothy with the job of leading the church and directing the people. Because Paul could not be there with Timothy, he

sent this letter as a sort of cheer. He included two kinds of cheers in his letter. Some told things he appreciated about Timothy and some listed things Timothy should do. He used the letter as a cheer to say, "you can do this job and here's how to do it." Timothy received the letter and followed its instructions with an "I think I can" attitude. He translated those cheers into positive statements about himself. Pretty soon "I think I can" turned into "I know I can!" and Timothy went on with his important job in Ephesus. Let's take a closer look at the book of Timothy to see some of the "cheers" Paul gave to Timothy.

Distribute copies of the activity sheet "Three Cheers for Timothy!" (page 40). Instruct the kids to complete the first section of the sheet by reading each Scripture passage and looking for the warnings and challenges Paul wrote to Timothy. Circulate around the room and offer help when needed. Review their findings from the passages listed. The list of warnings might include: Don't let anyone look down on you because you are young. Do not neglect your gift. Watch your life and doctrine closely. Challenges might include: Set an example. Devote yourself to. . . Be diligent. Persevere.

Then lead a discussion of what "I messages" Timothy could receive from those warnings and challenges. Some examples are:

- I am old enough to do this job.
- I have been given gifts from God.
- I can set a good example.
- I can read, preach, and teach.
- I can be diligent.

Put the kids in "cheerleading squads" of three or four students, and give them a few minutes to write a cheer for Timothy. Let them perform their cheers for the rest of the class.

 Living the Lesson (5-10 minutes)

We've talked about how cheers are an example of sending and receiving positive messages. Our Unit Verse is a great example of God cheering us on by telling us how He feels about us. Let's say it together. Lead the kids in saying the verse together several times.

Have each cheerleading squad take a paper with a Scripture reference from the container and design a way to say all or part of that verse as a cheer from God to us. Then have each squad present its cheer to the rest of the class.

Close today with a prayer of celebration, thanking God for believing in us, and sending positive messages to us in His Word.

Strain That Brain! ✓

EXAMPLE:

NEGATIVE STATEMENT: You jerk, you missed the basket three times. Can't you do anything right?

STRAIN OUT THE JUNK! What NOT to say	SAY WHAT IS TRUE! instead
I'm a jerk. I can't do anything right. I can't play this game. Everybody is mad at me.	I'm not a jerk! I made a mistake. I can try harder. I can do lots of things right!

#1: I can't believe you're wearing that shirt with those pants. What a combination!

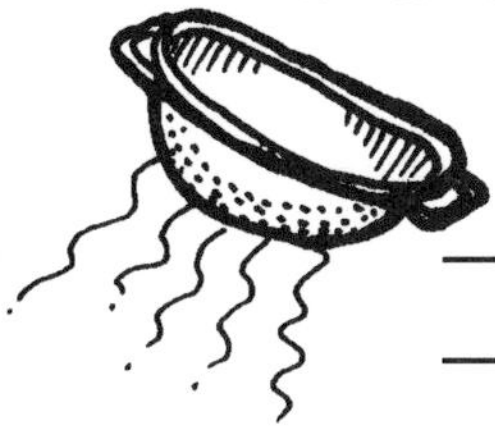

STRAIN OUT THE JUNK!   **SAY WHAT IS TRUE!**

_____   _____

_____   _____

_____   _____

#2: You only got a C on your report. I thought you could do better than that.

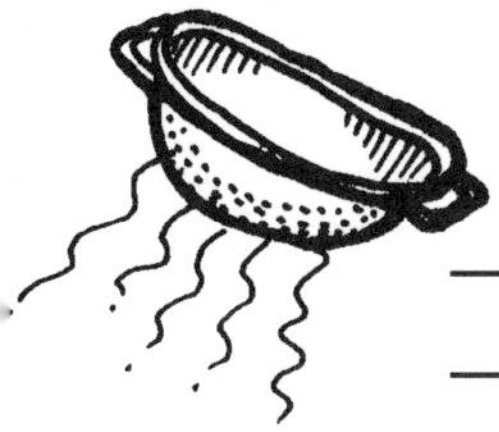

STRAIN OUT THE JUNK!   **SAY WHAT IS TRUE!**

_____   _____

_____   _____

_____   _____

#3: Only nerds bring their lunch to school in a bag. What a geek!

STRAIN OUT THE JUNK!   **SAY WHAT IS TRUE!**

_____   _____

_____   _____

_____   _____

#4: I wish you would listen once in a while. Do I always have to repeat myself? You never listen.

STRAIN OUT THE JUNK!   **SAY WHAT IS TRUE!**

_____   _____

_____   _____

_____   _____

"Three Cheers for Timothy!"

Cheers that warned

I Timothy 4:12 _____

I Timothy 4:14 _____

Cheers that challenged

I Timothy 4:11 _____

I Timothy 4:13 _____

I Timothy 4:15 _____

"I think I can!" statements

_____

_____

Make up your own cheer for Timothy. Write it here.

_____

_____

_____

Lesson 5

Awesome Adolescence

Aim: That your students will understand and accept physical and emotional changes as normal parts of God's plan for growing up.

Scripture: Psalm 139:1-4, 13, 14

Unit Verse: You are precious and honored in my sight, and . . . I love you. Isaiah 43:4

Unit Affirmation: I CAN LIKE MYSELF!

 **Planning Ahead**

1. Photocopy Activity Sheets (pages 47 and 48)—one for each student.
2. Prepare two pieces of poster board or shelf paper with the words, ACCOMPLISHED ALREADY at the top of one and TO DO LIST at the top of the other. Attach them to the walls at an appropriate height for students to write on.
3. **OPTIONAL:** Invite someone to give a short knitting demonstration.

1 Setting the Stage (5-10 minutes)

WHAT YOU'LL DO

- Compare responses to show how we grow and change at different rates

WHAT YOU'LL NEED

- "Growth = Change" Activity Sheet (page 47)

2 Introducing the Issue (20 minutes)

WHAT YOU'LL DO

- **OPTIONAL:** Play a game to show how rate and size of growth differs
- Explore the changes of our own growth
- Add a phrase to the Unit Affirmation poster

WHAT YOU'LL NEED

- Facts about growth
- Unit Affirmation poster

3 Searching the Scriptures (20 minutes)

WHAT YOU'LL DO

- Decode Bible verses showing how God created and knows us
- **OPTIONAL:** Watch a demonstration illustrating how carefully and wonderfully God has created us

WHAT YOU'LL NEED

- "Programmed for Success" Activity Sheet (page 48)
- **OPTIONAL:** An invited guest to present a knitting demonstration

4 Living the Lesson (5-10 minutes)

WHAT YOU'LL DO

- Make a list of things already accomplished and a to do list for the future

WHAT YOU'LL NEED

- ACCOMPLISHED ALREADY and TO DO LIST poster boards

Setting the Stage (5-10 minutes)

As children arrive, give each one a copy of the activity sheet "Growth = Change" (page 47). Instruct them to read each statement and color the corresponding section with the color indicated to make the statement true about them. When all have arrived and completed their sheets, instruct them to circulate among the other class members and find the person most like them.

You probably discovered that no two of you are exactly alike. Over the years, you have grown and changed in many ways. You've grown taller, learned new things, and had many new experiences. You know that a new phase of growth is ahead of you. During that time, you will undergo some of the greatest changes of your entire life, both physically and emotionally. These changes might feel scary, especially when we look around and see that others are changing and growing differently than we are! Today we are going to look at how God has provided for us to grow and change according to His plan.

Introducing the Issue (20 minutes)

OPTIONAL: Divide the class into teams of four to six students and give the instructions for playing the following version of the game "Pictionary." Each team will send a player up to you to begin play. You will whisper the first word on the list in their ears. They will then go back to their team and begin to draw the object. They may not use any words or letters. When the team has guessed correctly, they send up the next person who must tell you the word (to verify the answer), and then receive the next one. The first team to guess all the words wins.

WORDS FOR PLAY
Redwood tree
Hair
Daisy
Butterfly
Panda
Fingernail
Elephant
Kangaroo
Baby Human
Camel
As the words are guessed by both teams, write them on the chalkboard or a

Lesson 5

large piece of paper. If you do not play the game, have the words listed on a large sheet of paper. **What things can you think of that all these words have in common?** Allow for responses. **Although there are many things they have in common, the main one we want to talk about today is: They are all things that grow and develop. Some grow quickly, others don't. Some have extremely long life spans and some don't live very long at all. Which thing on the list do you think takes the longest to develop and grow?** (The redwood tree.) **Which has the shortest life span?** (Daisy or butterfly.) **Each of these things has a unique way of growing and developing.**

    Let's make some comparisons about how things grow. Listen to the statement and guess what you think the missing number might be. Some of them may surprise you! Read the statement leaving out the number in it. Let the kids guess the correct number by calling it out. Reveal the answer and move on to the next statement.

1. A mother camel can have only one baby every (two) years.
2. People can have a baby approximately every (twelve) months.
3. Elephants weigh more than (200) pounds at birth and are about (3-1/2) feet tall. (Hope none of YOU were that big!)
4. A tiger is the biggest cat in the world. Fully grown it weighs more than (600) pounds and including its tail can be more than (10) feet long.
5. Pandas start out as mouse-size newborns but grow to over (100) pounds in about (18) months.
6. An 18-month-old child weighs about (15-20) pounds.
7. Redwood trees often reach heights of (300) feet and live for thousands of years. But they only grow a few inches a year.
8. Mother kangaroos have a pouch in the front of their stomach. After birth, baby kangaroos stay there for about (6) months. What a social life!

    Help your class realize that by examining all of God's creation, they can see that He had a special blueprint in mind for everything He created! Even within the same species, animals and people grow and develop at varying rates and to different sizes. God designed it that way. Growing is an amazing thing. Normal children vary greatly in the way they grow, both physically and mentally. Some are quick starters. They grow tall at an early age. Some learn to read and write much sooner than others. Each child develops at his or her own special rate!

    Growth doesn't take place at a steady rate, either. There are spurts during which you may grow quickly and there are other times when you don't seem to change much at all. Think about your growing up years so far. When did you go through your growth spurts? The first big growth spurt happens between 18 months and three years. After that, there is not much change until five to seven years. **Do you know when your next growth spurt will come?** Explain that the years of puberty bring growth

spurts at different times for boys and girls. This usually happens between the ages of 10 and 12 for girls and 12 and 16 for boys. **That's right about now for some of you. What are some of the changes you are facing now, or can expect to face in the near future?** Brainstorm some of these changes together as a class. Write their responses on the board. Be sure your list includes:

1) Bodily changes as maturity takes place.
2) Growth spurt, resulting in clumsiness as muscles stretch and grow, and sometimes muscle spasms.
3) Emotional changes as bodies begin to produce adult hormones. This can result in moodiness and rapid mood swings.
4) Change in feelings about the opposite sex. Enjoying making friends with the opposite sex enlarges and brings variety to our relationship circle.

Which of these changes feel the scariest to you? Allow for responses, encouraging the kids to talk freely about their concerns as they approach adolescence. **The next few years may feel awkward to you. It does for most everyone! But just remember one important point: Your growth process is as uniquely your own as your fingerprints we looked at several weeks ago! Remember, God is in control.**

Display the Unit Affirmation poster. Since this is the last week of the unit, review it carefully, noting how each phrase is an important step in liking ourselves. Ask students to think of a phrase they could add today, such as "by knowing God controls how I grow," or "by growing at my own pace." **Now let's take a look at some verses in the psalms that talk about God's plan for our growth.**

Searching the Scriptures (20 minutes)

Distribute copies of the activity sheet "Programmed for Success" (page 48). **What is a computer program?** (A program is a series of directions coded on a disk to tell the computer what to do, and how and when to do it!) **What would happen if you had a computer, but no programs for it?** (Without the program, a computer would be just a fancy looking box.) **God designed the program for each one of our bodies. Before we were even born, He prepared a detailed list of instructions for how our bodies should grow and develop. The messages are coded deep within our brains. At just the right time, our bodies produce hormones which go to the brain and "run the program" telling our bodies how to grow and change. It's like a secret code designed by God within our own body. Psalm 139 tells us about this process.** Allow time for your students to decode the words in this passage. The answers are: vs. 1 searched, know; vs. 2 sit, rise, thoughts; vs. 3 discern, lying, familiar, ways; vs. 4 tongue, completely; vs. 13

created, inmost, knit; vs. 14. fearfully, wonderfully, well. After they have completed the sheet, review the passage together.

What's the verb or action word in verse one? (Searched.) **Have you ever lost something really important? What was it and what did you do?** Let kids respond. **When you lose something valuable, you may look for hours for it! You become very familiar with the area in which you are looking. This passage tells us that God has searched us and knows us—every nook and cranny! He is familiar with every part of us, inside and out! Look at verses two through four. Let's make a list of all the things God knows about us.** Record the responses on the board. Possibilities are: When I sit, when I rise, my thoughts, where I go, when I sleep, all my ways, everything I say before I even say it! **There is no one in all the earth who knows you better than God.**

In verse 13 what does it say God created? (My inmost being.) **What do you think he is talking about?** (The inner physical part of a person, such as heart, liver, kidney. Also the soul, the part of the person that wants a relationship with God.) **This verse contains a wonderful word picture of how God has created us. How does it say God made you?** (Knit me together.)

OPTIONAL: Invite a guest to come and help the class understand this passage better. Introduce the guest and give time for the knitting demonstration. Possible elements to emphasize: It is a slow, detailed process. Each time the needle passes under the yarn, it makes one tiny stitch. Thousands upon thousands of these tiny stitches form one garment. Dropping a stitch can be disastrous, and ruin the whole thing! Good knitters are patient and give great attention to every detail of their pattern. Using a purl stitch when you should use a knit stitch upsets the whole pattern. But when it is done properly, and carefully, the finished product is beautiful, and can be used with great pride.

Can you picture God with a pair of knitting needles? Knit one, purl two! God didn't really sit down and make us with needles and yarn, but the idea gives us a picture of how He made us. We are each made of billions of tiny cells. Each one is dependent upon another. God made all of our intricate parts work together to make a unique individual. Our bodies are one of the most intricate designs in all of creation!

Point out that the next few verses in Psalm 139 tell about the quality of God's workmanship. **What words describe how He made us?** (Fearfully and wonderfully.) Explain to the kids that the word "fearfully" doesn't mean full of fear or scared. It means extremely. It is meant to add power to the word wonderfully. Some other synonyms might be awesome, incredible, or unbelievable.

These verses tell us that God knows everything about us. He knows us better than we know ourselves. He understands how our bodies work and how we feel. Nothing we say or do is a surprise to Him. At a time when you are going through great physical and emotional changes, this comes as super news! God understands the

frustrations you experience as your body changes and matures. When you experience frustration, fear, or uncertainty about the way your body is growing and changing He knows how you feel. You can talk to Him about it. Talking to God is one good way to handle the changes involved in growing up. Let's name some other ways we can make growing and changing easier. Ask for suggestions. Some ideas are: reading books to know what to expect, talking with carefully selected friends experiencing the same things, talking with respected adults who've already been through it.

On days when you feel overwhelmed by the changes taking place, it's reassuring to know that:

1. GOD IS IN CONTROL.
2. HE KNOWS YOU INSIDE AND OUT AND MADE A DISTINCT PLAN FOR YOUR GROWTH.
3. HE MADE YOU IN A WONDERFUL WAY.
4. NOTHING STAYS THE SAME FOREVER

Living the Lesson (5-10 minutes)

Changing and growing can bring temporary frustrations and mixed emotions. But there are many exciting things about growing up and maturing. Display the two poster boards on the wall, ALREADY ACCOMPLISHED and TO DO LIST. End your class by inviting the kids to spend time writing items on one board a list of things they have already accomplished since they were born, and on the other a list of things they are looking forward to accomplishing as they grow up and become adults. They can go back and forth as many times as they wish. If you have a large class, you might want to display several sets of the same posters. Circulate with your students, making suggestions as needed. Some possibilities are:

ALREADY ACCOMPLISHED	"TO DO" LIST
Sit up	Drive a car
Feed self	Having one's own apartment
Crawl	Having a family
Talk	Playing some high school sport
Learn alphabet	Go to college
Make friends	Getting a job

End today's session by thanking God in prayer for the way He made each one of us. Thank Him for caring enough to know every detail of our lives. Thank Him for the way each child has grown and matured up to this point. Ask God to be with each of your students in the coming years. Pray that He will continue to guide them in all they do. Pray that each child would remain in a close relationship to the Lord and depend on Him each day to help cope with our lifetime of changes.

Read each statement and color the space according to the statement that is true about YOU!

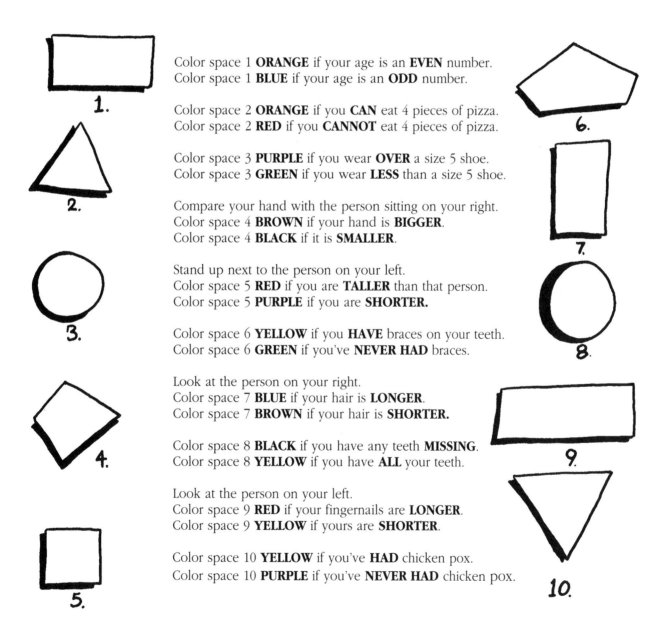

Color space 1 **ORANGE** if your age is an **EVEN** number.
Color space 1 **BLUE** if your age is an **ODD** number.

Color space 2 **ORANGE** if you **CAN** eat 4 pieces of pizza.
Color space 2 **RED** if you **CANNOT** eat 4 pieces of pizza.

Color space 3 **PURPLE** if you wear **OVER** a size 5 shoe.
Color space 3 **GREEN** if you wear **LESS** than a size 5 shoe.

Compare your hand with the person sitting on your right.
Color space 4 **BROWN** if your hand is **BIGGER**.
Color space 4 **BLACK** if it is **SMALLER**.

Stand up next to the person on your left.
Color space 5 **RED** if you are **TALLER** than that person.
Color space 5 **PURPLE** if you are **SHORTER.**

Color space 6 **YELLOW** if you **HAVE** braces on your teeth.
Color space 6 **GREEN** if you've **NEVER HAD** braces.

Look at the person on your right.
Color space 7 **BLUE** if your hair is **LONGER.**
Color space 7 **BROWN** if your hair is **SHORTER.**

Color space 8 **BLACK** if you have any teeth **MISSING**.
Color space 8 **YELLOW** if you have **ALL** your teeth.

Look at the person on your left.
Color space 9 **RED** if your fingernails are **LONGER.**
Color space 9 **YELLOW** if yours are **SHORTER.**

Color space 10 **YELLOW** if you've **HAD** chicken pox.
Color space 10 **PURPLE** if you've **NEVER HAD** chicken pox.

✔ Programmed for Success

PSALM 139: 1-4, 13 and 14

Decode the following words to complete these verses. Although the vowels have been given to you, and the telephone buttons can help you find the right letters, you will still need to decide between at least two letters that have the same number. Go for the challenge!!

code:

	ABC	DEF
1	2	3
GHI 4	JKL 5	MNO 6
PRS 7	TUV 8	WXY 9

verse 1

O Lord, you have 7-E-A-7-2-4-E-3 me and you 5-6-O-9 me.

_____   _____

verse 2

You know when I 7-I-8 and when I 7-4-7-E; you perceive my 8-4-O-U-4-4-8-7 from afar.

_____   _____   _____

verse 3

You 3-I-7-2-E-7-6 my going out and my 5-9-I-6-4 down; you are 3-A-6-I-5-I-A-7 with all my 9-A-9-7.

_____   _____   _____   _____

verse 4

Before a word is on my 8-O-6-4-U-E, you know it 2-O-6-7-5-E-8-E-5-9, O Lord.

_____   _____

verse 13

For you 2-7-E-A-8-E-3 my I-6-6-O-7-8 being; you 5-6-I-8 me together in my mother's womb.

_____   _____   _____

verse 14

I praise you because I am 3-E-A-7-3-U-5-5-9 and 9-O-6-3-E-7-3-U-5-5-9 made; your works are

_____   _____

wonderful, I know that full 9-E-5-5. _____

Service Projects for Self-esteem

Your class can use a variety of methods to help others feel better about themselves. This is a double blessing because as they do things for others they will receive a sense of accomplishment in return.

✔ 1. Adopt another class or a missionary family. Show support and care by writing letters of encouragement and sending "care packages" of special items selected just for them. Have everyone look for opportunities to encourage the adopted class or family in a variety of ways—telephone calls, visits, mail, or baked goods.

✔ 2. Make a banner communicating a self-esteem message to be displayed at the church or Sunday school. For example, you could print a computer banner with the unit verse, "You are precious and honored in God's sight!" and involve the kids in coloring and decorating it. Post it where the majority of the congregation will see their message. If your class is large, have small groups think of other messages to print and display.

✔ 3. Throw a "You Are Special" party! Pick a group within your church to honor and design a party just for them (group ideas could include seniors, a younger class, or families of class members). Design the menu, activities, and decorations with that specific group of individuals in mind. Use one of the games from this unit's lessons as an ice breaker.

Much More Alike Than Different

Junior-age kids are very concerned about what others think of them. Peer pressure condemns differences. As a consequence your Juniors are fearful of any kind of differences that would make them unacceptable to "the group." This anxiety also brings about extreme reactions to those who are dissimilar from them. All through history intolerance has played a big part in the persecution of individuals or entire groups of people. Today prejudice and hate crimes are growing societal concerns.

In this unit, you and your Juniors will explore four areas of differences. As you do, you will want to be sensitive to any stress your kids may be feeling about each of these areas and keep in mind that students who are different may feel threatened. However, this unit will give you an opportunity to reduce the fears and stress by encouraging your students to see beyond hasty generalizations of groups to individuals within them.

Through the use of the Unit Verse and the Unit Affirmation, you can assure them that God has made us all part of His body and challenge them to interact with people different from themselves. By creating an accepting and affirming environment you will help them comprehend that differences are not to be punished, but understood, accepted, and celebrated in Jesus' name.

✔ Differences Overview

Unit Verse: In Christ we who are many form one body, and each member belongs to all the others. We have different gifts, according to the grace given us. Romans 12:5, 6a

Unit Affirmation: I CAN ENJOY OTHERS WHO ARE DIFFERENT THAN I AM!

LESSON	TITLE	OBJECTIVE	SCRIPTURE BASE
Lesson #1	More Alike Than Different	That your students will understand what life is like for the disabled and handicapped and learn how to interact with them in a positive way.	II Samuel 9:1-13
Lesson #2	You've Got a Lot to Give	That your students will appreciate the God-given talents in themselves and others.	Genesis 30:1-21; Exodus 3:11, 12; I Samuel 16:23; 17:50; John 1:40; 6:8; Acts 9:36-39; I Timothy 1:1-3; II Timothy 4:11
Lesson #3	Family Trees Have Roots	That your students will appreciate the cultural differences of others and be proud of their own heritage.	Acts 11:1-18
Lesson #4	All God's Children	That your students will stop discriminating against others because of differences but instead, regard all people as special creations made in God's image.	Colossians 3:11-14

Partners

For the next few weeks your Junior-age child will be part of a group learning about Differences. *Partners* is a planned parent piece to keep you informed of what will be taught during this exciting series.

PREVIEW...

Differences

We are often wary of those who are different from us. Yet God created us with many differences. We come from different racial and cultural backgrounds. Added to these dissimilarities are differences in gender, age, and physical and mental abilities. We often make hasty generalizations based on first impressions. This leads us to avoid or dislike people simply because they belong to a particular race or other target group. In doing this we rob ourselves of relationships that can enrich our lives.

If your kids are like most Junior-age kids today, they are very concerned with what others think of them. They band together with those who are like them because this makes them feel safe. Any differences are a threat. Because they have not yet learned all the social graces, their responses to these differences may be extreme.

As parents and teachers, now is the time for us to help our children see prejudice for what it is. We can do this by assuring them that God considers all people as equal members of the human race and that He has given us to each other to enrich and strengthen us.

In the weeks ahead, your kids will learn that differences are best handled by taking time to look beyond first impressions and getting to know individuals. By affirming and accepting those who are unlike themselves they will find that differences not only make life interesting, but also help us appreciate it more fully!

Unit Verse:

In Christ we who are many form one body, and each member belongs to all the others. We have different gifts, according to the grace given us. Romans 12:5, 6a

Unit Affirmation:

I CAN ENJOY OTHERS WHO ARE DIFFERENT THAN I AM!

PRINCIPLES...

Differences

This unit will help your child learn several basic principles about differences:

PRINCIPLE #1:
GOD HAS CREATED EACH OF US DIFFERENTLY.

This principle is being taught each week through the first part of the Unit Verse, Romans 12:5.

Your kids will be learning that the disabled are more like us than they are different. They will develop a new understanding of the daily difficulties the disabled must overcome and see some of the ways society has handicapped them. At the same time, they will be encouraged to learn how to interact with the disabled in positive ways.

PRINCIPLE #2:
WE ARE TO USE OUR DIFFERENCES TO STRENGTHEN ONE ANOTHER.

By making a survey of the gifts and skills they admire in others they will be better able to express their appreciation to people who have and use their God-given gifts to strengthen and expand the outreach of God's family.

PRINCIPLE #3:
ALL PEOPLE ARE GOD'S SPECIAL CREATIONS AND BELONG TO EACH OTHER.

As they are learning to rejoice in their own cultural roots they will also be learning how to appreciate the various ethnic heritages of others. In today's world millions of new refugees are pouring into established national populations. Old ethnic boundaries have disappeared and more than ever before, the world has become a melting pot of international neighbors.

As our children grow up in this atmosphere they need to know that differences are interesting and enriching, and non threatening. Your kids will be encouraged to develop a regard for all people as special creations made in God's image. This will help them gain a new attitude of understanding and acceptance toward those who are different.

PRACTICE...
Accepting and Appreciating Differences

You can take an active role in helping your kids overcome

prejudice and reach out in acceptance in Jesus' name. Here are a few ideas to get you started:

1. CREATE AN ACCEPTING ENVIRONMENT IN YOUR HOME.

As you talk with your children daily, make individual affirmation a primary focus. Acceptance by others is one of the major concerns for Junior-age kids. Although they are related, family members still differ greatly from each other. No two people have identical talents and personalities. The family can be a safe area where the uniqueness of members is noted while still affirming them as special creations made in God's image. When kids feel accepted and affirmed in their homes, they are better able to cope with the differences of others.

2. PLAN ACTIVITIES THAT GIVE FRESH INSIGHTS INTO THE PROBLEMS OF THE DISABLED.

Take the family on a tour of public buildings to see first-hand the obstacles disabled people encounter daily. Make notes of entrances with heavy doors, no access routes for wheelchairs, restrooms with

narrow stalls, out-of-reach sinks or mirrors. Put yourselves in the place of people with walkers, crutches, wheelchairs or poor vision as you take a ride on public transportation. Developing a sensitivity to the disabled is an important part of helping them to be all God wants them to be.

3. BECOME ACQUAINTED WITH PEOPLE FROM OTHER CULTURES.

Invite these people to your home for meals. As you learn about their food, customs, and families, you can develop an appreciation for them and the differences that make life interesting. Pray for them as individuals for whom you, and God, care a great deal.

4. INCLUDE HOLIDAY CUSTOMS OF OTHER CULTURES.

As a family, research celebrations in other ethnic groups. Let your kids enjoy some of these such as a Hispanic piñata for a birthday party or a Japanese fish-kite for Children's Day.

5. PLAN AN INTERGENERATIONAL FAMILY GATHERING.

Because of changing family styles, children often miss the understanding and appreciation gained through extended families. If your family is without grandparents, adopt some from a local retirement center or through your church. Include them in family activities.

Lesson 1

More Alike Than Different

Aim: That your students will understand what life is like for the disabled and handicapped and learn how to interact with them in a positive way.

Scripture: II Samuel 9:1-13

Unit Verse: In Christ we who are many form one body, and each member belongs to all the others. We have different gifts, according to the grace given us. Romans 12:5, 6a

Unit Affirmation: I CAN ENJOY OTHERS WHO ARE DIFFERENT THAN I AM!

 **Planning Ahead**

1. Photocopy activity sheets (pages 59 and 60)—one for each student.
2. Prepare the Unit Affirmation poster by writing across the top of a large posterboard the words: I CAN ENJOY OTHERS WHO ARE DIFFERENT THAN I AM! Under the title write the numbers 1-4 vertically down the left-hand side.
3. Write the following words on separate pieces of small paper: BLIND, DEAF, ONE LEG, ONE ARM, LEGS PARALYZED, ARMS PARALYZED. Make as many copies of these words as necessary for each student to have one. Fold the papers and put them in a container.

1 Setting the Stage (5-10 minutes)

WHAT YOU'LL DO

- Play a game of Challenges to experience some disabilities

WHAT YOU'LL NEED

- Scarves, or other cloth for blindfolds—enough for half the number of students in your class

2 Introducing the Issue (20 minutes)

WHAT YOU'LL DO

- Discuss different disabilities and the difficulties and challenges they cause
- Use an activity sheet to act out how to be a friend
- Introduce the Unit Affirmation poster

WHAT YOU'LL NEED

- "Helps or Hinders?" Activity Sheet (page 59)
- Unit Affirmation poster

3 Searching the Scriptures (20 minutes)

WHAT YOU'LL DO

- Discover how a king showed kindness to a disabled man
- Make a list of attitudes toward others

WHAT YOU'LL NEED

- "Consider Yourself Part of the Family" Activity Sheet (page 60)

4 Living the Lesson (5-10 minutes)

WHAT YOU'LL DO

- **OPTIONAL:** Invite a guest to share some physical or mental challenges
- Plan ways to interact with disabled people in helpful ways

WHAT YOU'LL NEED

- **OPTIONAL:** poster board or large sheet of paper, marker

Setting the Stage (5-10 minutes)

As your kids arrive, have them take from the container a paper with a physical challenge written on it. This is to be their physical condition for this activity. Those who are paralyzed are to act accordingly. Those who have the words BLIND and DEAF are to put on scarves and headphones to make their condition realistic.

We're going to play a game similar to Simon Says. It's a different kind called Challenges. In this game you will play as you would play Simon Says, but with some physical limitations. Take your limitation seriously, but do the best you can. Choose a leader or lead the game yourself.

After play has continued for several minutes have kids remove their blindfolds and headphones and sit down. **How did you like this game?** (Reactions will be mixed.) **How did it compare to regular Simon Says?** (It was harder, not as much fun.) **Why?** (Couldn't see where you were going, was confusing, felt helpless, out-of-touch with other players.) **How is this similar to life for people who have physical difficulties such as these?** (They often have the same feelings, life is harder for them.) **How is playing the game different?** (We can take the blindfolds off, they can't stop being blind, deaf, without limbs, or not paralyzed.)

Introducing the Issue (20 minutes)

For the next four weeks we will be talking about differences. What kind of a world do you think it would be if everyone was exactly like you? What if they all looked like you, ate what you did, played the same games, or talked the same way you do? (Reactions may differ from wonderful to boring.) Point out that life wouldn't be as interesting or as much fun.

The truth of the matter is that God didn't make us all alike. Being different means we are very special creations. No one is exactly like you. Some of these differences can be seen easily. Point out some of the diversities in your students such as hair or eye color, height, freckles. Be sensitive to kids who may be concerned about not feeling they have the group's approval. Kids at this age want to be accepted and anything that sets them apart may be frightening. **All these differences are what make you unique and very special. You are an original!**

Some people have physical differences like blindness or not being able to hear very well. These differences create challenges for these people to be able to do what they want to do. They are referred to as "physically disabled" individuals. What are some of the challenges a blind person may have? What about the challenges of someone who only has one arm? Give

Differences

Lesson 1

some examples such as high curbs or steps for a person in a wheelchair or a roomful of obstacles for someone who is blind. **Can you name some other disabilities?** (Not being able to walk, speech disorder, mental or learning problems, paralysis.)

Be sure kids understand some of the terms used for disabilities such as: Blind—unable to see; deaf—unable to hear; learning disabilities—unable to see letters or words correctly; speech problems—stuttering, lisping, unclear speech; paralysis—unable to use arms and/or legs; cerebral palsy—sudden spasms of muscles that make walking, handling things, or talking difficult; mental retardation—unable to learn and develop normally; mute—unable to make sounds or talk. **What disabilities did you feel when you played the game today?** (Being blind, deaf.)

Focus kids' attention on the sameness of the disabled to able-bodied persons. Even though they have physical challenges, disabled people are exactly like those of us without those challenges. They have likes and dislikes, enjoy being with people, want to do all the same things you want to do, have feelings of anger and joy.

Many times the biggest challenges disabled people face are people's attitudes toward them. This may prevent them from enjoying life and living it to their full ability. Sometimes we don't realize we handicap them. Other times we may do it on purpose.

Distribute copies of the activity sheet "Helps or Hinders?" (page 59). Read the directions together. Allow a few minutes for kids to mark their answers. Answers are: help, help, hinder, hinder, help, hinder. Form six groups and give each one of the situations on the activity sheet. Have them demonstrate the way to be a friend in each case.

Knowing the best way to help someone who is disabled is also the best way to realize how you are really alike. You can be a part of that person's life and also make things easier for him or her. When we *insist* on doing things for disabled people, we really prevent them from doing things they can and want to do for themselves. It makes them feel helpless. It is like saying to them, "You aren't equal to me. You can't be expected to do much because you're disabled." By offering our help we leave them the option of accepting, redirecting, or rejecting it.

Why do you think we ignore or avoid disabled people? (We are uncomfortable and don't know what to expect or how to interact with them.) **Did it help when you experienced some physical challenges yourself?**

Display the Unit Affirmation poster and read it aloud as a class. **Disabled people are not sick or helpless. They are more like us than they are different. Always remember, Jesus wants you to help them be the very best they can be.** Let kids suggest phrases to add to the poster then choose one similar to "by treating all others as I would like to be treated." Write this after the number one.

Now let's take a look at God's Word to see how a king showed kindness to a disabled man.

✓ Searching the Scriptures (20 minutes)

Distribute copies of the activity sheet "Consider Yourself Part of the Family" (page 60). You will read the story aloud, pausing so students can pantomime each section as describe in the parentheses. For example, when you read "David promised to always be a friend to Jonathan," "David" pretends to promise "Jonathan."

Before you read the story, make sure everyone is involved in the skit. Assign these parts: David, Jonathan, Ziba, Mephibosheth, Makir, David's servant(s), son(s) and servant(s) of Ziba. Explain that Mephibosheth was crippled in both feet so the person playing him should remain seated in a chair or on the floor. Read the story while the group does the appropriate pantomime.

Talk about the story after you have read it. Mephibosheth was crippled because he was dropped by his nurse when he was only five as they tried to escape their enemies. (See II Samuel 4:4.) In many places, people who are disabled become outcasts and beggars. In Mephibosheth's case a friend of his family, Makir, had kindly cared for him.

Turn to II Samuel 9:1-13. **How did Mephibosheth describe himself?** (Servant, dead dog.) Dogs were scavengers and looked down on as worthless pests. "Dog" was considered a term of contempt and used to describe bad people. A dead dog was worth even less than a live one!

Why do you think Mephibosheth called himself these names? (He was used to people treating him badly, he was afraid of David. As a part of the previous reigning family he feared for his life.) **How do you think he may have felt about himself?** (Worthless, sad, wished he wasn't disabled.)

How did David react to Mephibosheth's disability? (Treated him as a friend and the son of his friend Jonathan.)

What does the Bible say David did for Mephibosheth? (Gave him back his grandfather's land, appointed Ziba to farm it for him; made him part of his own family.) David could have ignored Mephibosheth or just assigned him a place to live and sent him food. Instead, he brought Mephibosheth into his home where he could talk and eat with him every day. This allowed Mephibosheth to maintain the dignity of doing what he could for himself (living a nearly normal life) while also providing someone (Ziba) to help him do what he could not do (farm).

How do you think Mephibosheth felt about David's kindness to him? (Surprised, like he was worth something, accepted and equal to other people.)

David's kindness is a good example for us to follow when we help the

disabled. One of the important things the disabled need is to feel good about themselves. They are not as concerned about special treatment as much as about being respected and accepted as worthwhile individuals.

How do you think the Israelites reacted to David's treatment of Mephibosheth? (Were surprised, thought it was weird and unusual, respected his example, began to think about how they could treat disabled people better.) David was a great favorite with the people so they would be closely watching his actions. This positive example of God's love reaching out through one of His children must have made a strong impression on them.

What can we learn from this story? (God wants us to treat everyone like we want to be treated.) David's example shows us how to interact with those who have challenges we don't have. Some principles of this can be drawn out of this story. You may wish to list these on the chalkboard or a large sheet of paper so everyone can see them.

1. **Don't ignore or avoid disabled people.** When David discovered Jonathan's son Mephibosheth existed, he sought him out and treated him like he would treat any other member of his friend's family.

2. **All people are special creations of God and should be treated with respect.** David respectfully called Mephibosheth by name and told Ziba he was his "master's grandson." Never once did he refer to Mephibosheth's disability, or let it influence their relationship.

3. **Find out what disabled people can and cannot do for themselves.** Offer to help them with the things they cannot do. David realized Mephibosheth would never be able to farm his own land, so he found a way it could be done for him.

4. **Make life as enjoyable and easy as it can be for them.** David probably instructed his servants to make life comfortable for Mephibosheth. This would include keeping obstacles out of his path, providing comfortable chairs and a bed, and probably some way to help him get around.

5. **Help the disabled to be all they can be by finding out what they want to learn to do.** By including him as a valued member of his family, David

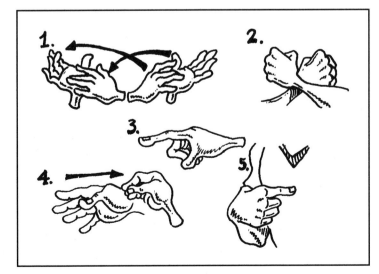

encouraged Mephibosheth to accomplish all that he could and restored his self-worth. The conversation with David's family and guests would provide intellectual stimulation for Mephibosheth and widen the tiny world his disability had enforced upon him.

Have students turn to Romans 12:5, 6a and read it together. **What do you think "Each member belongs to all the others" means?** (God made all people, we should take care of each other, treat others like we want to be treated.) **Every human being is a special creation of God. God's desire for us is to love and enjoy each other. This includes people who are different than we are.**

We're going to learn how to say "Jesus loves you and me" in sign language. This is the way some deaf people communicate. Demonstrate these signs to kids then have them do the signs with you several times.

✔ Living the Lesson (5-10 minutes)

> **OPTIONAL:** If you know a disabled person who is willing to share insights with your kids, invite him or her to be your guest.

Divide the class into small groups of two or three people. Let each group brainstorm ways to be sensitive and helpful to those who are different from themselves in some way. Some ideas are: talk about interests of people your same age; offer to carry, pick up, or reach things; plan events they can participate in; talk directly to them, not about them; become prayer partners with them; ask how you can best help. Assign someone in each group to write down the suggestions. Have them think of specific ways they might help individuals they already know.

After several minutes, regroup and have the teams read their suggestions. Write these on the board or a large sheet of paper. Remembering that disabled people are just like them is the biggest thing that will help your kids interact positively with them. We all suffer from limitations of some kind. Treat all people as you would like to be treated. Help them to be all they can be.

Have students pray silently, asking God to help them act toward other people in a positive, understanding way. Close by repeating "Jesus loves you and me" in sign language.

Helps or Hinders?

Look at each of the situations below. Decide if it is a way to help the disabled person or if it is really hindering that person. If you think it is helpful, circle HELP. If you think it may be hurting and hindering, circle HINDER. Then write an explanation or a way you can turn a HINDER into a HELP.

1. Chris is deaf. You want to say something to him so you look directly at him and speak slowly.
(HELP - HINDER WHY?)

2. Jenny has cerebral palsy. She wears a leg brace and has trouble carrying things. You offer to carry her lunch tray.
(HELP - HINDER WHY?)

3. Mark stutters when he tries to talk. You say the words for him.
(HELP - HINDER WHY?)

4. Maria is blind. She's waiting to cross the street. You grab her elbow and pull her across.
(HELP - HINDER WHY?)

5. Galan uses a wheelchair. He wants to hang up his jacket, but the rack is out of reach. You offer to hang it for him.
(HELP - HINDER WHY?)

6. Vicki is mentally disabled. She says something to you, but you can't understand it. You walk away and ignore her.
(HELP - HINDER WHY?)

CHARACTERS: David, Jonathan, Ziba, Mephibosheth, Makir, David's servant(s), son(s) and servant(s) of Ziba

Many years ago, David was best friend's with Jonathan, the son of King Saul. David promised to always be a friend to Jonathan and all the members of his family. (David promises Jonathan.)

Now King Saul was dead and David was king. His best friend Jonathan was also dead, but David asked his servants if there were any members of Saul's family still alive. (David asks his servants.) The servants told David that one of Saul's servants named Ziba might know. David sent his servants to bring Ziba to him. (David sends servants to Ziba. Servants bring Ziba to David.)

The king asked Ziba if there was anyone left from Saul's family so he could show kindness to him. Ziba told him that Jonathan's son, Mephibosheth, was still alive. Mephibosheth was crippled in both feet and lived with a man named Makir. (David and Ziba talk.)

King David quickly sent his servants to the house of Makir. (David sends servants to Makir.) The servants told Mephibosheth that King David wanted to see him. (Servants talk to Mephibosheth.) It was the custom for new kings to kill all the sons and grandsons of their enemies so Mephibosheth was afraid David would kill him. The servants helped the disabled man come before the king. (Servants help Mephibosheth come to king.) Mephibosheth fearfully bowed down to honor David. (Mephibosheth bows down.)

David happily welcomed Mephibosheth and told him not to be afraid because he only wanted to be kind to him. (David welcomes Mephibosheth.) The king gave the disabled man the land that had belonged to his grandfather, Saul. Then he invited him to live with David's family in the palace.

The king sent his servants to bring Ziba to him. (King sends servants to Ziba.) They bring him to David. He told Ziba to farm the land for Mephibosheth and use the food to take care of the crippled man and his family. Ziba took his sons and his servants and helped the disabled man by farming the land for him. (Ziba, his sons, and servants go farm land.)

From that time on, David treated Mephibosheth like one of his own children. He took special care of him because Mephibosheth was Jonathan's son. (David takes care of Mephibosheth.)

God wants all of us to be kind to disabled people in the same way David was kind to Mephibosheth. (Everyone gathers around David and Mephibosheth.)

You've Got a Lot to Give

Aim: That your students will appreciate the God-given talents in themselves and others.

Scripture: Genesis 30:1-21; Exodus 3:11, 12; I Samuel 16:23; 17:50; John 1:40; 6:8; Acts 9:36-39; I Timothy 1:1-3; II Timothy 4:11

Unit Verse: In Christ we who are many form one body, and each member belongs to all the others. We have different gifts, according to the grace given us. Romans 12:5, 6a

Unit Affirmation: I CAN ENJOY OTHERS WHO ARE DIFFERENT THAN I AM!

 **Planning Ahead**

1. Photocopy Activity Sheets (pages 67 and 68)—one for each student.
2. Cut paper circles large enough for a student to stand in. Make one for each student.

1 Setting the Stage (5-10 minutes)

WHAT YOU'LL DO

- Interview others to talk about gifts

WHAT YOU'LL NEED

- "Talent Search" Activity Sheet (page 67)

2 Introducing the Issue (20 minutes)

WHAT YOU'LL DO

- Discuss gifts and recognize that everyone is gifted by God
- Add a phrase to the Unit Affirmation poster

WHAT YOU'LL NEED

- Apple and banana
- Unit Affirmation poster

3 Searching the Scriptures (20 minutes)

WHAT YOU'LL DO

- Find out ways several Bible people used the gifts God gave them to honor Him and help others

WHAT YOU'LL NEED

- "Bible Talent Show" Activity Sheet (page 68)
- One 3" x 5" card for each student

4 Living the Lesson (5-10 minutes)

WHAT YOU'LL DO

- Make a survey of gifts admired in others and express appreciation for them
- Recognize the source of our gifts

WHAT YOU'LL NEED

- Notecards and envelopes
- Paper circles

Lesson 2

✓ Setting the Stage (5-10 minutes)

As the students arrive, distribute copies of the activity sheet "Talent Search" (page 67). Have them interview several people, using the questions on the activity sheet. Be sure that everyone is interviewed at least once. The results from these interviews will be used later in the lesson.

God has given each one of us special talents or gifts. People have different gifts so we can work together to help others and honor God. We can appreciate the talents He has given us and also those of others. Today we're going to talk about some of these gifts.

✓ Introducing the Issue (20 minutes)

Many people who do not possess obvious talents like singing or painting think they don't have any gifts or abilities. Not all talents are flashy or visible. Sometimes the least showy talents are the most valuable. We need farmers and factory workers as much as executives and artists.

Gifts are special abilities that God gives to us. Just as muscles grow when we exercise and use them, so our gifts grow and develop into something useful as we use them. A person may have a gift for gymnastics. If she or he finds a good coach to help, does exercises, and practices many hours a day, the gift becomes usable. When that person uses that ability to help mentally retarded kids train for Special Olympics God is honored and others are helped.

How do you know what gift God has given to you? A good way to determine your gift is to notice the things you enjoy doing, the kinds of things others ask you to do, and what you are complimented on. Give students some examples: **Do you like to visit with older people or little children? Do you like to help others accomplish a task? Do you enjoy playing games and sports and teaching others how to play? Do teachers or other adults give you responsibility to take care of things? Do your friends talk to you about their problems?**

We often can't see our own gifts as well as we can see those of others. Have students share some of their interviews from SETTING THE STAGE. Discuss some gifts that may have been overlooked such as being friendly, caring for nature, working well with others, doing thoughtful things for others, mechanics or carpentry, crafts, cooking. All of these talents are gifts from God.

Think about the information listed for you. It may give you an idea of

possible gifts God gave you. Are there some things listed you didn't consider as gifts? Have them share some of these things. This helps other students rethink their own talents.

Not everyone has the same talents. Your friend might play the piano beautifully while the only thing you can play is the radio. Maybe you are super at helping strangers feel welcome in class while your piano-playing friend is too shy to do that. Sometimes we feel that our gift isn't very important. We wish we had the gift someone else has.

Display the apple and banana. Trying to compare our gifts with others is like trying to compare apples and bananas. Each fruit is delicious and useful, but they are quite different.

Briefly discuss ways gifts and skills can be used to help others and honor God. **Let's say Bill liked to build model rockets, identify bugs, help little kids, and go on camping trips.** List these on the chalkboard or a large sheet of paper. **How could he use these talents in his home?** (Help his parents out with younger brothers or sisters; plan a family camping trip.) **How could he use them in church?** (Be a helper for a younger class for VBS or Children's Church, an assistant for a camping trip for younger kids.) **What about in school?** (Help someone with a science project, playground assistant, be a school crossing guard.) **How could Bill use these same talents for the less fortunate?** (Be a "Big Brother" to some little kid in a homeless shelter, help out in a day camp or day care center, get a lonesome kid started in an interesting hobby.)

Display the Unit Affirmation Poster and read the Affirmation aloud together. **God has given each one of us at least one talent. This wonderful gift is what makes every person a special, original creation. What phrase can we add to the next line of our poster?** Let kids make suggestions. Choose one that says something like "when I appreciate their talents and develop my own." Write this on the second line.

Let's look at some Bible people who discovered they were not only talented but could develop skills by using their gifts to honor God and help others.

✓ Searching the Scriptures (20 minutes)

Distribute copies of the activity sheet "Bible Talent Show" (page 68). This is done like an interview program with seven mystery guests and a host. Choose

someone to be the host and guests. In order to include more participants, have each mystery guest choose a partner to be his or her publicity manager. If you have a large class, create additional supporting roles so each student is a part of a group for each guest. Have each group look up their verses on the activity sheet before the interview program begins. In some cases have the Publicity Manager or another member of the guest's entourage present the information about the guest. Set up chairs for the guests and place the host in the center. Use a disconnected microphone or even a big spoon for a "mike" to add to the fun!

After the presentation of the interview show, discuss the activity together. **What was a common problem for all the "guests" in this drama?** (They all thought they didn't have any gifts.) **Why did they think that?** (Because they compared themselves with others.) Have kids give you some examples from the skit. **How did the people in the skit solve the problem?** (Realized God had given everyone, including them, a special and useful gift.) Stress the importance of this. God has given everyone at least one gift. That includes each of your students!

Sometimes we have the same problem these Bible people had. Who are some people kids your age might envy because of their talents? Let students share some real-life examples they face such as measuring themselves with kids who are prominent in school sports, are smart, or excel in music or art. Because they are so influenced by media and entertainment people, kids might also mention some of these "super-stars." **Why do you want gifts that are equal to theirs?**

Ask two kids to read aloud I Corinthians 12:7 and 14:12, 26. **Why did God give us talents?** (Build up and strengthen the church, for the good of others.) Stress that the "church" is not a building people meet in, but a group of people who are followers of Jesus. **Does this change your thoughts about which gifts are the most important? If so, how?** Point out that because we aren't to use them for ourselves, but to help each other, the more important gifts are those that enable us to do that.

Let's take a look at some of the Bible passages used in the skit again. What did the people mentioned in these verses do with their skills? Have kids look up these passages if they have not done so earlier. (Worked at improving them, used them to help others, honor God.) **What are some examples of how they did this?** Let students share these. David is a good example. He rid Israel of one of its enemies when he killed Goliath with his slingshot, but before he took on the giant, David announced he was doing it so "the whole world will know that there is a God in Israel" (I Samuel 17:46b).

David also wrote some of the psalms which have been, and continue to be, a source of blessing to countless people in times of sorrow and trouble.

Training and using our gifts makes them more usable. The saying "no pain, no gain!" is as true in developing skills and gifts as it is in training our muscles for sports or good health. A musical gift can be turned into a skill such as playing the piano, but there's a long period of scales and finger exercises between discovering the gift and playing for a singer or church service which honors God and blesses others.

Have students turn to Romans 12:5, 6a and read the unit verse aloud together. **What does our Unit Verse say about gifts?** (We have different gifts.) **Who gave them to us?** (God.) Re-emphasize that God gave us these gifts so we could use them to honor Him and help others. We should be willing to dedicate our gifts to God's service and not use them selfishly for personal gain or success. Distribute index cards. **Choose one gift you think you have and write it at the top of your card. Think of a way you can use the gift this week to honor God. Write it on the card and plan to do it.**

> **OPTIONAL:** To help your kids develop and use their talents, they could present the Interview skit for another class. This could also be done with puppets taking the parts rather than the students themselves. Instead of individually writing down the names of the mystery guests, your class could make it into a game by having the audience identify the guests aloud.

✔ Living the Lesson (5-10 minutes)

Give a sheet of paper to each student. Ask them to write "Gifted People" at the top of the page and then divide the paper into three columns labeled: PERSON, GIFTS, HOW USED. Under the title of the first column write the numbers one-three vertically.

Write down the names of three people who have gifts and skills you admire. Then write down the gift or skill and how the person uses it to honor God and help others.

> **OPTIONAL:** Distribute the notepaper and envelopes. Choose one person from your list and write a brief thank you to him or her.

A dedication service is a good way to close today's lesson. **It has been said that "What we are is God's gift to us. What we become is our gift to God."**

Here is an opportunity for you to give your special gift back to God.
Distribute paper circles. Tell the class to place their circles on the floor. **If you know that God has given you your talents to be used to honor Him and help others then step into the circle.** Allow time for your Juniors to silently pray an individual dedication prayer. You may prefer to have your students take their circles home and make their dedications privately.

Close with a prayer of thanksgiving for each student.

Talent Search ✓

Write in your name as the Interviewer, read over the interview questions, and then find someone to interview. Write the responses on this paper.

INTERVIEWER: _____
Questions:

1. What are some things you enjoy doing? Consider things such as hobbies, free-time fun.
2. What are some things you think you are good at?
3. What are some things you receive compliments about? List these things.

Interviewee #1

1._____
_____
2._____
_____
3._____
_____

Interviewee #2

1._____
_____
_____
2._____
_____
_____
3._____
_____
_____

Interviewee #3

1._____
_____
_____
2._____
_____
_____
3._____
_____
_____

Bible Talent Show

HOST: Welcome to Bible Talent Show. Today we have a terrific line-up of mystery guests who will tell us about their gifts from God and how they used them to help others. Let's see if you can name each person. Here's Guest #1.

GUEST 1: I wasn't a good public speaker like my older brother, but God promised to be with me and gave me the gift of leadership. I used it to free God's people from their enemies and lead them out of slavery. My name is_____. (Exodus 3:11,12)

HOST: Wonderful! Guest #2, what was your gift?

GUEST 2: I was the older daughter and not very attractive. Because of that, my father tricked my husband into marrying me instead of my beautiful younger sister. In spite of this trick, I loved and

trusted the Lord. I taught my seven children to do that also. One of my sons became an ancestor of Jesus. My name is_____. (Genesis 29:16-27)

HOST: Love and trust give spiritual beauty. You used those gifts to honor God and He blessed the world through you. Guest #3, please tell us about yourself.

GUEST 3: My father felt I was unimportant. My seven older brothers thought me a bothersome little pest, but God gave me the gift of music. I wrote, sang songs, and played my harp while I was alone with my sheep. I also developed perfect aim with my slingshot. Those skills helped me to kill a giant, entertain a king, and write a book of hymns. I'm_____. (I Samuel 16:23, 17:50)

HOST: God certainly gave you many gifts. Let's hear from our next guest.

GUEST 4: Whenever I met people who needed God I told them about Jesus and introduced them to Him. That's how my outspoken brother became a follower of Jesus. Once I brought a little boy to the Master and He used the boy's lunch to feed five thousand people. My name is_____. (John 1:40, 6:8)

HOST: Being a friend is an important gift as you discovered. Guest #5, what gift did God give to you?

GUEST 5: I gave up and went home in the middle of a vital missionary journey. The apostle Paul called me a quitter and wouldn't let me go with him anymore, but my uncle saw that I had the gifts of being a writer and helper. Through his encouragement I used those gifts and wrote a book about the life of Jesus. Later, Paul said I was a real help to him and asked for me to assist him personally. I'm_____. (II Timothy 4:11)

HOST: That was quite a turnaround for you. Guest #6 please tell us about yourself.

GUEST 6: I was quite shy and sickly. I felt I just didn't measure up to my famous Christian friends. The apostle Paul saw that I had gifts from God to become a church leader. I trusted God to help me and became the pastor at the city of Ephesus. I'm_____. (I Timothy 1:1-3)

HOST: Great! Now for our last guest. What was your gift?

GUEST 7: I wanted to help needy people, but all I could do was sew. I developed the skill so I could make clothes for many poor widows and orphans. I'm _____. (Acts 9:36-39)

HOST: Good for you! There you have it. Whatever your gift is you can use it to help others and honor God.

Lesson 3 ✔

Family Trees Have Roots

Aim: That your students will appreciate the cultural differences of others and be proud of their own heritage.

Scripture: Acts 11:1-18

Unit Verse: In Christ we who are many form one body, and each member belongs to all the others. We have different gifts, according to the grace given us. Romans 12:5, 6a

Unit Affirmation: I CAN ENJOY OTHERS WHO ARE DIFFERENT THAN I AM!

 **Planning Ahead**

1. Photocopy Activity Sheets (pages 75 and 76)—one for each student.
2. Attach a world map to the bulletin board or wall. Have available small Post-it notes or map tacks.
3. Using travel magazines and other sources, collect a variety of pictures of persons of all ages of as many different nationalities as possible.
4. Make a Graffiti Wall by writing WHO ARE WE across the top of a 6 - 8 foot piece of shelf paper. Write SAME on the left side of the paper and DIFFERENT on the right side. Attach this to the wall at an appropriate height for your students to write on.
5. Ask the parents of your students to give their children some family background to assist in discussing cultures.

1 Setting the Stage (5-10 minutes)

WHAT YOU'LL DO

• Create a Graffiti Wall of human similarities and differences

WHAT YOU'LL NEED

• WHO ARE WE Graffiti Wall
• Pictures of persons from many different nationalities

2 Introducing the Issue (20 minutes)

WHAT YOU'LL DO

• Participate in a survey to discover different cultural backgrounds
• Add a phrase to the Unit Affirmation Poster

WHAT YOU'LL NEED

• "Tracing My Roots" Activity Sheet (page 75)
• Unit Affirmation poster

3 Searching the Scriptures (20 minutes)

WHAT YOU'LL DO

• See how an opinionated man learned to appreciate people from a different cultural background

WHAT YOU'LL NEED

• "Love in Any Language" Activity Sheet (page 76)
• **OPTIONAL:** One 3" x 5" card for each student

4 Living the Lesson (5-10 minutes)

WHAT YOU'LL DO

• Explore ways to celebrate cultures

WHAT YOU'LL NEED

• WHO ARE WE Graffiti Wall

✔ Setting the Stage (5-10 minutes)

As the students arrive, have them attach the pictures you have of persons of different nations to the top of the Graffiti Wall. Then have them write as many different things to each side of the wall SAME and DIFFERENT as possible. As necessary, suggest some things such as emotions, inside a person, the outside appearance of a person, foods, language, games.

We can appreciate cultures different than ours and add more enjoyment to our own lives by stopping to think about the people. How are we alike? How are we different?

✔ Introducing the Issue (20 minutes)

Opening our relationships to include others who are different than we are makes life interesting and lets us enjoy it more. To help us appreciate other cultures, we need also to discover our own. The more personal details we learn about our family roots the more pride we can take in our heritage. Distribute the activity sheet "Tracing My Roots" (page 75). Have kids read the directions aloud together. After working for a few minutes have the kids share their answers. If students are unable to trace their roots to a particular culture, they can fill in the rest of the information (holidays, food, toys/games, and crafts) with things they enjoy.

How many of you know where your ancestors lived? How many cultures do we represent? List these on chalkboard or large sheet of paper. **Is one country represented more than others? If so, which one?** Have students put a map tack or a Post-it note on their ethnic country on the world map.

Do any of you know any words from your cultural or historical language? If anyone can speak or write something in their ancestral language, encourage them to share these words with the group. Perhaps some of the families still speak their national language and the kids are bilingual. Talk about their feelings about knowing more than one language. Is it fun? Helpful? A problem or embarrassment? Where families are still fairly new immigrants, children learn their new homeland's language faster than their parents. This often places them in the role of interpreter.

Look at the national costumes you listed. Does the country your ancestors came from have anything to do with these? How? (Hot countries mean less or more loose clothes; cold countries require more clothes and

different fabrics.) **Did the type of weather or land have anything to do with how your ancestors made a living for themselves?** (Fishermen, farmers, traders, nomad shepherds.)

Which holiday is the favorite of our group? Many of the holiday customs celebrated in this country originated somewhere else: Christmas tree (Germany); fireworks (China); new Easter clothes (early Christians in the Middle East). Most of your students will find their celebrations are a collection of several cultures.

How many have eaten food that is from a different country? Although they may not realize it, almost everyone has experienced another culture through the food they eat. Talk about this common experience. **What are some foods that came from another country?** Some examples are: tacos, French bread, bananas, and chewing gum. **Does your family have a special food they eat for celebrations? If so, what is it?** Examples are lutefisk—Scandinavia and bankeletter/Dutch letters—The Netherlands.

How much do you think we would be missing today if we didn't learn about and appreciate cultures that are different than us? What kinds of things would be omitted? (Food treats; inventions that make our lives better such as the bicycle–France, safety match–Sweden, and the X-ray machine–Germany; famous writers–C.S. Lewis and Apostle Paul; artists–Rembrandt and Michelangelo; athletes like Jim Thorpe–Native American, and Eric Liddell–Gr. Britain.)

Display the Unit Affirmation poster. Read it together aloud. **Taking pride in our own heritage helps us see ourselves and our family in new ways. We realize how important our family roots are. This leads us to discover the wonderful resources other cultures add to our lives. These differences are what make life interesting. What phrase can we add to the next line of our poster?** Have kids offer their ideas. You might choose one like, "when I value the things their cultures add to my life," or "by learning to appreciate their family roots." Write this on the third line.

One Bible man felt that only his own cultural group was important to God. Let's find out what he learned about people who were different than he was.

✓ Searching the Scriptures (20 minutes)

Distribute copies of the activity sheet "Love in Any Language" (page 76). Ask someone to read the directions aloud. Have students work at this in pairs or groups of three.

Answers are: kill, eat, Lord, impure, unclean, God, clean, three times, pulled,

heaven, three men, Caesarea, hesitation, six, house, angel, Joppa, Simon Peter, message, you, Holy Spirit, them, us, the beginning, the Lord, John, you, Holy Spirit, God, Lord Jesus Christ, God, God, repentance.

After the blanks are filled in, read this play aloud. Assign kids to take the parts of Peter, the Voice from heaven, the Holy Spirit, angel, and Jesus. The part of the Jewish believers could be read in unison by a group.

Discuss the passage together. Be sure kids understand the key words used in this passage. Impure or unclean was used to describe people, animals, or actions that were not pleasing to God. God had told the Jews there were some animals they could not eat. These were called unclean. Jews called Gentiles (and non-Jews) unclean, meaning they could not be accepted by God. Jewish believers in Jesus thought the good news was intended for Jews only. A clean person was acceptable to serve God and was pleasing to Him.

Why did the Jewish believers criticize Peter? (He had gone to a non-Jewish home and eaten with the people there.) **According to what Peter said in the drama why did this upset them?** (They felt only Jews were pleasing to God; if Gentiles became believers, they had to obey Jewish customs.) This was a big area of debate among the Jewish believers. Some of them felt only Jews could be saved. Others accepted Gentile believers if they would obey the Jewish laws and traditions.

Do you think we ever feel that way toward people who are different? If so, how do we act toward them? Help kids see that they are showing the same kind of prejudice the Jews had when they ignore, exclude from friendships, and make fun of others because they are different.

Who did Peter bring with him when he appeared before the Jewish believers. (Six fellow believers who had gone with him to Caesarea.) **Why do you think he wanted them to come along?** (They saw and heard what God had done, would back him up.)

Peter was the ideal person for God to use to change the thinking of these Jewish believers. In Joppa, he was staying with Simon, a believer who was a tanner. Simon handled dead animals in order to get the skins he then prepared for leather. This occupation was considered "unclean" by the Jews because a dead animal should not be touched. Peter laid aside his prejudice with difficulty and probably stayed in Simon's house because of his love for Jesus. In this way he was prepared for the vision he had from God while he was there.

Why do you think God sent this vision to Peter? (To show him that God loved all people and didn't think the non-Jews were "unclean.") Have someone read Genesis 18:18 aloud. **From the beginning, God's plan for the Jews was to use them to bless all people.**

Ask another student to read Malachi 1:11. **What does God want all the**

world's people to do? (Praise, worship, pray to Him.) **What do these verses show us about how God feels about people who are different than ourselves?** (Includes them in His love and plans.)

Give some background information to help kids understand who Cornelius was. He was a Roman centurion. That meant he was an officer in charge of one hundred soldiers. The men he led were top-quality troops who kept the peace at the fort in Caesarea. Cornelius was well-respected by his men and the Jews. He learned all he could about God, worshiped Him, prayed to Him, and helped others who were in need. Only one thing was lacking in his life—he didn't know about the salvation Jesus had provided for all people. God planned to solve that problem by providing Peter to give Cornelius the information he needed to gain eternal life. At the same time God would open the eyes of the Jews to His plan for people of all nations.

What happened while Peter was telling Cornelius and his family the good news about Jesus? (The Holy Spirit was given to them.) **What did this teach Peter?** (God loves and accepts everyone who believes in Jesus and obeys Him.)

Have students say the Unit Verse together. The early church members learned that God has no favorites and never hides from those who seek Him. Differences in skin color, nationality, language, customs, money, age, or sex are not barriers to God. Anyone can be a member of His family by receiving forgiveness of sins through Jesus' death and a life spent living for Him. Ask the group to repeat the phrase "In Christ we who are many form one body."

OPTIONAL: Distribute index cards and have kids illustrate this phrase on it. If time permits, they can share these.

After his experience with Cornelius, Peter learned to appreciate people from a different cultural background. He accepted them as Jesus had accepted him.

✔ Living the Lesson (5-10 minutes)

Brainstorm together ways kids can celebrate their own cultures and that of others. The group is to come up with as many ways as possible. Have several kids write down the ideas on the chalkboard or a large sheet of paper. Some ideas are: learn more about your own roots by asking family members, try a food from another culture, play a new ethnic game, have a world's fair or meal and ask people from your church to help you make international booths or

prepare foods from their different cultural backgrounds. Use the WHO ARE WE Graffiti Wall for more ideas.

> **OPTIONAL:** Close by learning the phrase "Jesus loves me" in one or more languages. If one of your students knows a different language, ask him or her to teach some words to the others. Examples of "Jesus Loves Me" are: Spanish-"Cristo me ama" (KREE-stoh may AH-mah); Japanese—"Wa-ga shu E-su" (WAH-gah shoo, YAY-soo); Telegu language of Southern India—"Ye-su pre-ma gop-pa-di" (YAY-soo PRAY-ma gup-PAR-dee).

Tracing My Roots ✓

Ethnic groups are made up of people who share the same culture, language, ancestry and maybe national origin. Fill in as much information about yourself as you can. If you don't know the answer, skip it and go on.

1. First name, middle name, last name, nickname
_____

2. Country of my ancestors; Country from which my family came
_____

3. Ethnic group of my ancestors (Czech; Hmong; Zulu)
_____

4. Language they spoke; Language/s my family speaks today (Swahili; Spanish; French)
_____

5. Ethnic greeting my ancestors used or my family uses (Hola; Sayonara)
_____

6. National costume
_____

7. Ethnic holiday(s) my family celebrates
_____

8. Favorite holiday; When holiday is celebrated
_____

9. How we celebrate this holiday
_____

10. Special holiday foods we eat
_____

11. Favorite ethnic food my family enjoys
_____

12. Special ethnic custom/s my family celebrates (Quincerano—fifteenth birthday for Hispanic girl; Japanese tea ceremony)
_____

13. Ethnic crafts we do (Paper flowers; origami; Ukrainian Easter eggs)
_____

14. Games or toys our people group enjoys (piñata; tangram; soccer)
_____

Love in Any Language

Finish this play about Peter by reading Acts 11:1-18. Write in the correct information. Clues to the people and speeches are given for you. The first one is done for you as an example.

SCENE: Jerusalem, where the Jewish believers are criticizing Peter for associating with Gentiles (non-Jews).

PETER: Friends, I understand why you are upset. Until recently I also felt that only Jews were pleasing to God. Like many of you, I thought that Gentile believers should obey Jewish customs, but God showed me that that was not His plan. Let me explain. (vs. 4) While I was praying in Joppa I had <u>a vision.</u> A <u>sheet</u> came down from <u>heaven</u> and was lowered very near me. Inside it were (vs. 6) <u>wild beasts, reptiles, and birds.</u>

VOICE: Get up, Peter. (vs. 7)_____ and _____.

PETER: (vs. 8) No, _____! I have never eaten anything that's_____ or _____.

VOICE: (vs. 9) _____ made these things _____.

PETER: This happened (vs. 10) _____then the whole thing was _____ to _____. Right then (vs. 11) _____ came to the house where I was staying. They had been sent to me from _____.

THE SPIRIT: Go with them and have no (vs. 12) _____.

PETER: These (vs. 12) _____ believers also went with me and we entered the _____ of a man named Cornelius. He told us how he had seen an (vs. 13) _____ standing in his house. This angel talked to him.

ANGEL: Send some men to (vs. 13) _____ for _____ and invite him to come. He will bring you a (vs. 14) _____ that will save _____ and all your household.

Peter: When I began to speak, (vs. 15) the _____ came on _____ just as He had come on _____ at _____. Then I remembered what (vs. 16)_____ said.

JESUS: (vs. 16) _____ baptized with water, but _____ will be baptized with the _____.

PETER: Since (vs. 17)_____ gave them the same gift as He gave us who believed in the _____. Should I oppose _____? No!

JEWISH BELIEVERS: We should stop arguing. Let's praise (vs. 18) _____. He loves the Gentiles also and is giving them _____ and eternal life. We should also tell others who are different than we are the good news about Jesus and accept them as fellow believers in the Lord.

Lesson 4

All God's Children

Aim: That your students will stop discriminating against others because of differences but instead, regard all people as special creations made in God's image.

Scripture: Colossians 3:11-14

Unit Verse: In Christ we who are many form one body, and each member belongs to all the others. We have different gifts, according to the grace given us. Romans 12:5, 6a

Unit Affirmation: I CAN ENJOY OTHERS WHO ARE DIFFERENT THAN I AM!

 **Planning Ahead**

1. Photocopy Activity Sheets (pages 83 and 84)—one for each student.
2. Use six different colors of paper to make playing pieces for a Value game. Cut 1" squares of the different colors of paper. Make enough so each student will have four pieces.

1 Setting the Stage (5-10 minutes)

WHAT YOU'LL DO

• Play a game to discover the meaning of discrimination

WHAT YOU'LL NEED

• Game pieces for a Value game

2 Introducing the Issue (20 minutes)

WHAT YOU'LL DO

• Use an activity sheet to uncover ways of discrimination
• Add a phrase to the Unit Affirmation poster

WHAT YOU'LL NEED

• "Caution! Deceitful Discrimination" Activity Sheet (page 83)
• Unit Affirmation poster

3 Searching the Scriptures (20 minutes)

WHAT YOU'LL DO

• Learn what God's Word says about how we should treat those who are different from us

WHAT YOU'LL NEED

• "Colossian Chronicle" Activity Sheet (page 84)
• One 3" x 5" card for each student

4 Living the Lesson (5-10 minutes)

WHAT YOU'LL DO

• Make a frieze to appreciate the differences of others

WHAT YOU'LL NEED

• Variety of colored paper 8 1/2" x 11"—one sheet for each student

✓ Setting the Stage (5-10 minutes)

As kids arrive, give each one four squares of different colors to play the Value Game. Tell them the colors are worth different values. Students can swap with each other and collect the colors they think most valuable. Ask them to consider reasons why one color has a higher value than the others and write down their reasons. Don't reveal the values until game ends. After a few minutes of play, stop the swap. Select one color and announce that because it is the most valuable it is worth ten points. All the other colors have no value at all so only the ten-point color will be counted. Have the kids total the number of squares they have of that color. The player with the most points wins.

How did you feel about the way the most valued color was chosen? (It didn't make sense, confused, angry, you treated us unfairly.) **What are your reasons for choosing a certain color? Would you have swapped differently if you had known only that color would count? Why or why not?** (Yes. I wouldn't have wasted time collecting other colors.) **Suppose I asked you to make a rainbow picture using only the color I chose. Could you do it? Why or why not?** (No. A rainbow is made up of many different colors.)

The decision I made in the game based on my reason for choosing one color is much like discrimination. Today we want to talk about this problem.

✓ Introducing the Issue (20 minutes)

Write DISCRIMINATION and PREJUDICE on the chalkboard or a large sheet of paper. **What do these words mean?** (When we discriminate against others, we ignore their true worth and treat them differently just because they are not the same as we are.) Help kids understand that this is more than expressing personal likes and dislikes. Discrimination and prejudice are expressed in two ways. One is being unkind or mistreating others who are different than we are. Another is playing favorites, being more kind to some people, generally those who are like us. Discrimination is a sneaky, invisible poison that brings fear, unhappiness, and even death to people.

Distribute copies of the activity sheet "Caution! Deceitful Discrimination" (page 83). **This activity sheet gives some examples of the hidden way discrimination creeps into our lives and spoils them.** Have someone read the directions aloud. You're going to be detectives whose job is to uncover these tricky methods. The answers are: 1. mock; 2. ignore; 3. name-calling;

Lesson 4

4. physical abuse; 5. generalize or stereotype.

Ask someone to read the first example aloud. **Have you ever had someone make fun of you? How did it make you feel?** (Awful, stupid, worthless, angry.) **Mocking others who are different may seem like fun to the person doing it, but it is definitely not fun to the one who receives it. This is a common form of put-down.** Many times kids can't help being different. A parent's loss of a job, a divorce, or catastrophic illness can place tremendous financial burdens on a family. Birth defects or disabilities can't always be cured. Making fun of kids in these difficulties only adds to their troubles and creates low self-esteem.

Create four groups of students and assign each group one of the items on the activity sheet. Have each group solve its puzzle and then prepare to act out its type of discrimination. Discuss each type after it is presented.

Have group one present its skit. **One of the hardest treatments to endure is to be ignored. What do you feel like when that happens?** (Like I'm invisible or not even there, worthless, I want to do something, anything, to get attention!) **When people have been constantly ignored they will try to gain attention. This can lead to everything from individual discipline problems or suicide attempts to group riots or even wars.**

Have group two present its demonstration. **A cliche says "Sticks and stones may break my bones, but words can never hurt me." Do you agree or disagree with that? Why or why not?** (Most kids will disagree. Name-calling is another form of put-down. It hurts terribly.) Names tend to stick and countless adults have spent their lives trying to live down such damaging names as "Fatty," "Four-eyes," or "Stinky."

Have group three make its presentation. **Have you ever received this kind of treatment? Why would someone treat others like this?** (Fun, afraid someone would treat me like that someday.) **It's easy to get involved because others around you are doing it, but this form of prejudice not only causes great pain, but can also result in trouble with the law!**

Have the fourth group present its skit. **When we don't know people very well it is easy to generalize about them. That means we make a vague statement and apply it to a whole group.** Give an example. Suppose one kid in your class likes to eat chocolate–covered pickles. Does that mean all the kids in your class like chocolate–covered pickles? Of course not! Getting to know people who are different and appreciating them for their differences is the cure for such ridiculous thinking.

Ask kids to give you other examples of discrimination. No matter what type of discrimination is used, it hurts the person who is different. Just as sad is the truth that the person who discriminates against differences is robbed of rela-

tionships that could make life more enjoyable.

Display the Unit Affirmation poster. Read it together, including the previous phrases. Ask the group to think of a phrase they can add for today's lesson. Suggestions might be, "by considering each of them as God's special creation" or "when I learn to know them as individuals."

God's Word has some helpful hints on how we should treat those who are different from us. Let's find out what they are.

☑ Searching the Scriptures (20 minutes)

Imagine that you are living in the city of Colosse in the time of the apostle Paul. It is a city on the main trade route and includes people who differ greatly. It is about thirty years since Jesus went back to heaven. His followers have been telling others the good news of God's love and forgiveness.

Do you think they had discrimination then? Let kids give views. Help them understand that people then had the same problems and feelings people do today. **Let's find out what the local newspaper, the Colossian Chronicle, says about this.** Distribute copies of the activity sheet "Colossian Chronicle" (page 84).

Ask a volunteer to read aloud the top article. **What do you think people who were not followers of Jesus might have thought about the plan in this imaginary paper?** (Wouldn't work, curious, hoped it could change their lives.) If they treated others with discrimination this plan would cause reactions of anger and rejection. On the other hand, if they had been hurt by such treatment it might bring joy and hope.

How do you think believers in Jesus would feel about it? (Glad, weren't sure, encouraged, eager to do it.) **Would the poor and rich have felt the same? Why or why not?** (No, probably not.) At that time, there was no middle-class. It seemed the rich got richer while the poor got poorer. Ask someone to check out James 2:1-4 and read it aloud. **This Bible passage describes discrimination or partiality, based on clothing and appearances. One person looks wealthy. Does that mean he is more important?**

What does James call people who discriminated against others? (Judges with evil thoughts.) **Why do you think he calls them this?** Explain that when people discriminate they are really acting as judges who decide whether one person or group is better than another. This judgment is based on personal likes and dislikes and ignores an individual's worth as a person.

Have a volunteer read the article on the master and slave. This is a brief report of the reunion of Philemon and Onesimus, as it may have happened.

Philemon was a Greek-Christian landowner who lived in Colosse. The believers met in his home.

Gentile masters discriminated against their slaves. Slaves were not considered people, but "things." They had to do whatever the master told them and had no rights or choices. Perhaps this frustration is what led Onesimus to run away and hide in Rome. While there he met Paul and became a follower of Jesus. Paul sent the runaway slave home to Philemon. He was not just a slave now, but also a member of God's family.

As a master, Philemon had the legal right to kill his runaway slave, Onesimus. How do you think Onesimus felt about returning to his master? (Scared, nervous.) **Do you think people who have been discriminated against might feel the same way about having relationships with those who were unkind to them? Why or why not?** (No. They probably wouldn't be killed. Yes. They have been hurt and don't trust them.)

Why do you think Philemon welcomed Onesimus? (Because now they both loved Jesus.) Assign someone to read Philemon 9a aloud. **This verse gives us a tip on how to end discrimination. What is it?** (Love others.) Stress that this is the love of Jesus which fills our hearts and guides us in our treatment of others.

Ask someone to read the article on Paul. Have the class turn to Colossians 3:9-11. Although converts had been made in Gentile groups as well as Jewish, there was still a problem with discrimination. Paul wrote to the believers in Colosse to correct this obstacle to church unity. Colossians and Philemon were both written by Paul at about the same time. Colossians 3:11 must have meant a great deal to both Philemon and Onesimus. Their reconciliation proved that when Jesus' love controls our hearts, discrimination is banished and we can truly appreciate those who are different.

How should we treat others who are different than we are? (With compassion, kindness, humility, gentleness, and patience.) **How are we to treat those who have wronged us?** (No differently than we treat anyone else, forgive them as the Lord forgave us.) **What binds people together in perfect unity?** (The love of Jesus.)

When we ask Jesus to control our lives the differences among us aren't important anymore. Jesus is equally available to everyone. People differ in many ways, but God considers all the followers of Jesus, His Son, as equals. God created each of us special in His own image.

Have the group read the public opinion section silently. **You have read God's Word and thought about how we should treat others. Now write in your opinion in the space provided.** Assure kids that this is a private matter and will not be seen by anyone else.

Write DIFFERENCES on the board or a large sheet of paper. Have students say the Unit Verse together. Distribute index cards. **Each one of you is different and God works differently in your lives. Choose the part of this verse that means the most to you and write it on your card.** Encourage kids to take these home with them and use them as reminders of the wonderful, differing creations God has chosen to make in His image.

 # Living the Lesson (5-10 minutes)

We're going to make a frieze border decoration for our room to finish the study of this unit on differences. Distribute the paper, giving a separate 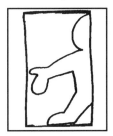 color to each student to accent the theme of differences. Have them fold the paper in half crosswise and then half again to make four sections. They should draw a figure next to the center fold similar to the illustration. Be sure the drawing extends to the edge of the paper for the connecting link for hands at the second fold. Cut the figure out. There are two identical figures with joining hands.

Let kids draw features on their paper people while you direct their thoughts to the previous lessons. Mention ways people differ (physically, culturally, age). Encourage students to complete their people to represent some of these differences.

Write ways you can appreciate the differences of others on your paper people. Emphasize that the suggestion should be as personal and specific as possible. Some examples are: Encourage my grandpa to tell about his childhood, Learn from my neighbor from Colombia how to make a wooden whistle.

Tape or staple the figures together to form a continuous border. Display it somewhere in the room. **No matter what the differences among us, each and every person is a special creation made in God's image. Jesus' love helps us appreciate our differences and still be members of God's family who serve and honor Him.** Pray briefly thanking God for the differences that make us special.

Caution! Deceitful Discrimination

Can you complete the pattern of the code so you can figure out the words? Check the clues for some hints, then use the code to unscramble the letters and uncover some of the ways we discriminate against other people. Write the correct word beside the scrambled one.

CODE:

A	B	C
D	E	F
G	H	I

J	K	L
M	N	O
P	Q	R

S	T	U
V	W	X
Y	Z	

Clues: A= ⌐   L= |•   S= ••   Z= |••

1. _____

"Get a load of those clothes! She looks like she got them out of the trash can."

2. _____

"Pretend you didn't hear that old man. He probably repeats everything anyway."

3. _____

"Heard you got another "D" on your book report. You're a real dummy!"

4. _____

"Let's beat up that new kid. That'll teach him not to try to join our team!"

5. _____ *and* _____

"Choose Caleb to be on your team. Everybody knows Blacks are great basketball players!"

©1992 David C. Cook Publishing Co. Permission granted to reproduce for classroom use only.

COLOSSIAN CHRONICLE

COLOSSE, ASIA MINOR   May 18, 60 A.D., 5 shekels

Group Announces Unique Plan!

The new religious group called "Christians" announced they will accept all believers in Jesus as equals, regardless of race, job, age, or wealth.

"Jesus' love and forgiveness breaks down all divisions," a leader said. "His love will bind us all in perfect unity." If put into action, this plan could change the world.

PAUL: No difference because Christ is in all believers:

The apostle Paul said today that followers of Jesus should "bear with each other and forgive as the Lord forgave you." He also urged Christians to love each other because that is what holds believers together in perfect unity.

At the same time, the missionary urged God's people to show mercy to others, be kind, humble, gentle, and patient because they were chosen, holy, and dearly loved.

Paul said there is no room for prejudice in the lives of Christians. Asked what he meant, he explained that there is no difference between Greeks or Jews, people who are foreigners or Scythians.

This comment has upset citizens because the Scythians are known as very wild and cruel people. Will lepers and beggars also be included? Where do we draw the line?

Paul repeated, "Christ is all, and is in all."

Master Welcomes Slave as Christian Brother

Philemon, rich landowner, has forgiven his former slave, Onesimus, and accepted him back as an equal. Onesimus ran away after being suspected of theft. "I asked God and Philemon to forgive me," he said. Philemon welcomed him and said, "I accept Onesimus in Jesus' love."

Public Opinion Poll

Today's question: "Would you treat those who are different than you as an equal?"
Demas: Not if that includes the poor. **Esther:** With God's help I could even accept and love a Persian.
Centurion Brutus: If they aren't Roman citizens, why should I? **YOU:** (Your opinion) _____
_____

Service Projects for Differences

✓ 1. Plan a trip to a retirement center to get acquainted with some of the residents. Prior to going, create a board game with about ten questions such as "How many brothers and sisters do you have?" or "What is your favorite food?" on some of the spaces. When players land on these spaces they have to answer the questions. Make several copies of the game for students and residents to play. Both the students and residents will develop a new appreciation for those who are different in age and life-styles.

✓ 2. Choose a way to celebrate several cultures in one event. For example, students could invite kids from other cultures to a pot-luck picnic. Have everyone bring a favorite food so you can have a "cultural sampler." Play games from the cultures represented.

✓ 3. Have the class take a survey of your church or school facilities to see how convenient they are for the disabled. Make a list of any improvements that need to be made. Meet with the trustees or custodians and share your list with them. With permission and the proper instruction, have a work day to do things such as placing soap or mirrors at a lower position.

✓ 4. Plan a "Celebrate God's Gifts" fair and have tables set up where students and other members of your church or school family can demonstrate their gifts. You could have displays of hobbies, crafts, and nature (plants and animals). People gifted in cooking could offer samples and those with musical skills could present a program or background music. People with child-care gifts could offer to do that during the fair so parents can be free to enjoy the displays.

✓ 5. If you know of people who are hearing impaired or speak a different cultural language, have students learn several songs and Bible verses in sign language or the cultural language. Invite guests to teach some sign language or a different spoken language. Share these with the appropriate people.

Who's the Boss?

Authority—it's something we all have to learn to live with! No matter if we are seven or seventy, we all have people and agencies in authority over us. Whether it is a teacher at school or the IRS, we all need to understand the role authority plays in our everyday lives!

How your Juniors learn to respect and obey authorities now can make a lifetime difference for them. That's why in the weeks ahead you will help your students discover what life would be like without leaders to guide and protect them. You will involve them in surveying the traits of good leaders and learning the danger signals to help recognize inappropriate leadership. As they study the Unit Verse and review the Unit Affirmation each week, they will understand the importance of obeying those God has placed over us. You will also have the opportunity to talk with your class about issues surrounding those times when they must learn to say no to those in positions of authority and protect themselves by getting help from other trusted adults. At the end of this unit, you will have the privilege of pointing your kids to the greatest authority they can have in their lives—Jesus Christ. As they examine the reasons why Jesus is our only completely trustworthy authority, you can help them make a commitment to Him as the ultimate authority for every part of their lives.

 **Authority Overview**

Unit Verse: Remind the people to be subject to rulers and authorities, to be obedient, to be ready to do whatever is good. Titus 3:1

Unit Affirmation: I CAN FOLLOW THE AUTHORITIES IN MY LIFE!

LESSON	TITLE	OBJECTIVE	SCRIPTURE BASE
Lesson #1	Why Do We Have to Have Authorities?	That your students will understand that God has given us authorities to help guide our lives.	Genesis 41:33-43, 53-57
Lesson #2	Who's the Boss?	That your students will identify characteristics of good authorities and show respect to the authorities in their lives.	Titus 1:6-9
Lesson #3	To Do or Not To Do	That your students will learn that God wants us to obey authorities except in matters of personal safety or when it is against God Himself.	Matthew 8:5-10, 13
Lesson #4	Head Over All Things	That your students will recognize that Jesus has all the characteristics of a good leader and deserves to be our ultimate authority.	John 10:7-18

Partners

F or the next few weeks your Junior-age child will be part of a group learning about Authority. *Partners* is a planned parent piece to keep you informed of what will be taught during this exciting series.

PREVIEW...
Authority

Authority—it's something we all have to learn to live with! No matter if we are seven or seventy, we all have people and agencies in authority over us. It doesn't matter if it is a teacher at school or the IRS, to get along in this world we all need to understand the role authority plays in our everyday lives! The way your children learn to respect and obey authorities now will make a lifetime difference for them. Whether it's a scout leader, a teacher, a coach, or you, they can learn principles of relating to authority figures that will help them be successful in the days and years ahead.

During this unit, your children will discuss what life would be like without authorities. They will survey traits of good leaders and learn the danger signals of

inappropriate leadership. As they study the Unit Verse and review the Unit Affirmation each week, they will understand the importance of obeying those God has placed over us. Finally, at the end of this unit they will hear about the greatest authority they can have in their lives—Jesus Christ. As they examine the reasons why Jesus is our only completely trustworthy authority, they will have an opportunity to make a commitment to Him as the ultimate authority for every part of their lives.

Unit Verse:

Remind the people to be subject to rulers and authorities, to be obedient, to be ready to do whatever is good. Titus 3:1

Unit Affirmation:

I CAN FOLLOW THE AUTHORITIES IN MY LIFE!

PRINCIPLES...
Authority
PRINCIPLE #1:
GOD HAS GIVEN US AUTHORITIES TO HELP GUIDE OUR LIVES.

Have you ever stopped to consider what this world would

be like without authority? Picture a world without traffic lights or police officers. Think about how your work place and home would change. And how about the church? Without people willing to accept authority, the church would grow stagnant and inoperable. No matter what the arena, we all need authorities to help guide us and give direction.

As your kids examine authority from world leaders to the authority figures in their own homes, they will discover that God's instruction to obey authorities was given in our best interest and with good in mind. They will see that obeying authority, even when they may not feel like it, can actually improve the quality of their lives.

PRINCIPLE #2:
I CAN SHOW RESPECT FOR AUTHORITIES.

Some people think that respect for authority is "going out of style." In a nation where freedom of speech may be escalated into the right to publish everyone's failures and shortcomings, it's sometimes hard to keep sight of the fact that most authorities do deserve our respect.

In the weeks ahead your children will survey characteristics of good authorities and name ways to show respect. They will be involved in writing several letters of thanks and encouragement to various authority figures, as well as identifying other ways of respecting the leaders in their lives.

PRINCIPLE #3:
GOD WANTS ME TO OBEY AUTHORITIES EXCEPT IN MATTERS OF PERSONAL SAFETY OR WHEN IT IS AGAINST GOD HIMSELF.

Although the biblical principle of obedience to and respect for authorities in our lives is still sound, we must acknowledge that we live in a world where children may be abused by authority figures. Children are often the innocent victims of sexual, physical, or emotional abuse. No unit on authority could be complete without exploring the boundaries of absolute obedience. Your child needs to know when it is right to disobey and how to get help when it is needed. To teach this concept, children will be taught two basic principles: Children should never be forced to do something

#1—that is against God's law or the law of the land.

#2—that hurts others or themselves.

During this discussion, your children will study some of God's laws and our nation's laws and see how they are designed to protect and promote a better life. They will talk about the difference between obeying this kind of appropriate authority, and authority that is inappropriate. Kids will be

warned that when a person in authority deliberately involves them in something inappropriate or hurts them, they are to say no and find a trusted adult to help.

PRINCIPLE #4:
JESUS IS THE PERFECT LEADER AND DESERVES TO BE MY ULTIMATE AUTHORITY.

If authorities are designed to make life better, guide us, and bring safety and security to our lives, who could surpass Jesus as the perfect authority? Jesus loved each one of us so much that He was willing to die for us. By making Him our ultimate authority, we receive the wealth of God's love, direction, guidance and protection into our lives.

During this unit, your child will have an opportunity to make a commitment to Jesus as his or her lifetime authority! By submitting and obeying Him, your child can look forward to a life filled with God's richest blessings!

PRACTICE...

Authority
1. DO A SELF CHECKUP.

What kind of example are you setting for your child? Do you constantly belittle your boss or slow down on the highway only when you see a police officer? Do you point out the strengths of political leaders as well as their weaknesses? By showing respect for those in authority over you, you provide your children with

a powerful role model for dealing with authorities in their own lives.

2. MEMORIZE THE UNIT VERSE.

Make this a family project. The verse presents a great reminder of common ground regardless of age. We are all subject to rulers and authorities.

3. BE AN INVESTIGATIVE REPORTER.

Choose an authority in your community, state or nation. Judges, council members, church leaders, and political leaders are all possibilities. Research how that person gained the position he or she now holds. Make a list of characteristics needed to perform the job or hold the position. If you can, find a way to meet with this person and do a personal interview. Then write a note of encouragement to that person expressing thanks for doing a sometimes difficult job.

4. TEACH AUTHORITY BY DELEGATING IT!

The best way to learn authority is to have it! Pick a few new jobs or responsibilities for your child to try out this month. It could be anything from learning new babysitting skills to grocery shopping for the entire family. Be creative as you and your child talk about the possibilities. Be sure to be available to guide your child through the learning process of this newly chosen area of responsibility.

Lesson 1

Why Do We Have to Have Authorities?

Aim: That your students will understand that God has given us authorities to help guide our lives.

Scripture: Genesis 41:33-43, 53-57

Unit Verse: Remind the people to be subject to rulers and authorities, to be obedient, to be ready to do whatever is good. Titus 3:1

Unit Affirmation: I CAN FOLLOW THE AUTHORITIES IN MY LIFE!

 **Planning Ahead**

1. Photocopy Activity Sheets (pages 95 and 96)—one for each student.
2. Prepare materials for the Unit Affirmation poster, but do not assemble it. Have a poster board, letters for the words I CAN FOLLOW THE AUTHORITIES IN MY LIFE, and numbers 1, 2, 3, 4, 5.
3. Prepare the supplies for recipes as described in SETTING THE STAGE. Write the instructions for each activity on separate pieces of paper.
4. **OPTIONAL:** Make a transparency of the activity sheet, "Who's In Charge?" (page 95) and arrange to have an overhead projector set up. Or make a reproduction of the sheet on a poster board.
5. Print the Unit Verse on a poster board or large piece of paper.

 Setting the Stage (5-10 minutes)

WHAT YOU'LL DO

- Participate in an activity station to experience the results of a lack of authority

WHAT YOU'LL NEED

- Recipe supplies

 Introducing the Issue (20 minutes)

WHAT YOU'LL DO

- Follow appropriate instructions and recipes
- Discuss the importance of authorities in our lives
- Use an activity sheet to identify authorities in our world

WHAT YOU'LL NEED

- Activity centers as set up in SETTING THE STAGE
- "Who's in Charge?" Activity Sheet (Page 95)

3 **Searching the Scriptures** (20 minutes)

WHAT YOU'LL DO

- Observe how a godly man guided a nation through a time of hardship
- Name symbols and powers given to Joseph as a ruler of Egypt
- Introduce the Unit Verse

WHAT YOU'LL NEED

- "Pharaoh's #1 Man" Activity Sheet (Page 96)
- Unit Verse poster

 Living the Lesson (5-10 minutes)

WHAT YOU'LL DO

- Show respect for authority by writing a letter of encouragement to a leader in your country

WHAT YOU'LL NEED

- Stationery, stamps

✓ Setting the Stage (5-10 minutes)

Before class, set up three activity stations. Include the supplies to make three different items, but do not include the recipe or instructions.

As students arrive direct them to the stations, but do not tell them what to do. Explain that they are not to mix anything at this time, but are to decide among themselves what to do and how to do it. As students question you about what they are supposed to do, respond using phrases like, "I don't know," "I'm not sure," and "What do you think?". Then ask them to make a list of what they think the goal of the activity could be by identifying what the ingredients might be used for or what the letters might spell.

ACTIVITY STATION #1: Have these supplies available: poster board, letters, numbers, glue, ruler, paper, pencils. (See Planning Ahead.)

ACTIVITY STATION #2: Have these supplies available: measuring cup, crunchy peanut butter, raisins, orange juice, slices of bread, medium–sized bowl, knife, paper, pencils.

ACTIVITY STATION #3: Have these supplies available: measuring cup, smooth peanut butter, honey, powdered milk, water, medium–sized bowl, paper towels, paper, pencils.

When all have arrived and written some possibilities for the activity, talk about them. **What do you think should happen at this table?** Allow time for responses. **How did it feel to have all the ingredients but not have any instructions or guidance? What would have helped make these activities more fun?** (Instructions and someone to take charge and show them what to do.) **For the next few weeks, we will be talking about the importance of having people in charge, and what it means for us to respect and obey the people who have authority over us. Although sometimes we don't like having people tell us what to do, we will discover how having authorities in our lives actually makes life easier!**

Recipe for Raisin-Orange-Peanut butter Sandwiches: Ingredients: 3/4 cup crunchy peanut butter, 1/3 cup raisins, 1/3 cup orange juice, and slices of bread. Mix the filling ingredients together in a medium–sized bowl, and spread on five slices of bread. Cut into quarters and serve open face. (Makes 20 pieces, adjust amounts of ingredients to fit the size of your class.)

Recipe for Edible Play Dough: Ingredients: 1 cup smooth peanut butter; 1/2 cup honey; 1 small box of powdered milk. Mix peanut butter and honey together in a medium–sized bowl. Stir in powdered milk until mixture becomes the consistency of play dough and can be handled easily. Kids can model anything they want, and then eat it!

Lesson 1

☑ Introducing the Issue (20 minutes)

Write the word AUTHORITY on the chalkboard or a large piece of paper. **Without instructions and a leader, our learning centers were very frustrating. There was one important ingredient missing when you came into the room today. That ingredient was "Authority."** Ask kids to brainstorm ideas and definitions for the word "authority." Record their ideas on the board. Some possibilities are: someone in charge, a person or group of people with power, to command and be obeyed, an expert, someone whose knowledge and opinions command respect and obedience. **Regardless of how young or old we are, we will always have people in authority over us. These authorities influence us on many levels.**

Distribute copies of the activity sheet "Who's in Charge?" (page 95) and go through it together, using the transparency or poster board copy of the activity sheet. Have the overhead projector set up and ready before class. Each circle on the activity sheet represents a realm of authority. Begin with the largest circle which represents God. **There is only one "ultimate authority" in all the world! Who is it?** (God.) **What are some of the ways in which God is the ultimate authority?** (Designer and creator of the earth, set up natural laws of the universe, gives life to each one of us.) **But God's Word tells us that we are to be subject to other authorities as well. We'll see later that our Unit Verse is a direct command to submit to rulers and authorities. Let's take a look at this sheet and name some of the authorities God asks us to follow.** From the outside working in, the circles should be labeled: God, Country Leaders, State/Province Leaders, City Leaders, Church Leaders, School Leaders, Home Leaders.

As a group, fill in the headings and some specific names and positions within that category. Ask the following questions for each section: **Do you think these people have a direct impact on your everyday life? Why or why not? Do they affect your life more or less than the last category we talked about? What problems could arise without these people to give leadership and guidance? Our world runs more smoothly when we have people in authority to make decisions and set policies and rules. The same thing is true even in our own classroom. Let's go back and try those interest centers again! This time though, I will assume authority for the class and supply you with the needed instructions.**

Divide the class into 3 groups and assign one to each interest center. Distribute the recipes for the sandwich and play dough tables. Give the Unit Affirmation center a card with the phrase written out so they can complete the poster. After each group has completed their project, distribute the sandwiches

and play dough for all to enjoy.

Display the Unit Affirmation poster and read it aloud as a class. Ask the students to think of a phrase that describes one thing they learned today about living with authorities. Examples: to make life better, to guide me, or to help keep my world organized and safe. Choose one and write it on the first line. **Now let's look at a Bible character who had lots of experience with authority.**

Searching the Scriptures (20 minutes)

Joseph was next to the youngest of twelve boys. The Bible tells us that Joseph's father loved him the most. You may recall the story of the coat of many colors and the resentment it caused. Being one of the youngest in the family, Joseph knew what it was like to be under authority. Even though he was favored, he was also "low man on the totem pole" and often had to obey not only his parents, but his brothers.

When he was only a young boy, Joseph had a dream which most of your students will remember. Remind them of the dream (Genesis 37:5-11) in which the sheaves of grain in the field bowed down to his. **This dream represented the fact that someday Joseph's brothers would bow down to him. He also dreamed that the sun, moon, and eleven stars bowed to him. That dream represented the fact that his family would someday bow to his authority. Before that could happen, however, Joseph would have to submit himself to the authority, sometimes even cruel authority, of others.**

Briefly review the story of how Joseph's brothers sold him into slavery (Genesis 37:17-28). Remind the kids how he spent years as a slave for Potiphar and even spent time in prison (Genesis 39:1-20). **Being sold into slavery and put into prison are not exactly authoritative positions! It must have been hard for Joseph to believe his dream would ever come true! But Joseph understood the importance of obeying God by submitting to the authority over him, and while he was in prison, he established a reputation for being able to interpret people's dreams. That led him to be called upon to interpret a dream of the Pharaoh. It must have been hard for Joseph to be honest with Pharoah and tell him the bad news of the dream—that there would be a terrible, seven-year famine in the land. But Joseph gave Pharaoh the truth, and in return, God revealed to him a detailed plan of what to do. Let's see what that plan was.** Ask a volunteer to read Genesis 41:33-37 aloud. **Verse 39 tells us that Pharaoh picked Joseph for the job!**

Lesson 1

His faithfulness to God and the authorities under whom he served was finally rewarded!

Distribute copies of the activity sheet "Pharaoh's #1 Man!" (page 96). Instruct students to decipher the pictures to discover how to complete the sentences. All phrases describe the power and authority given to Joseph. It also lists the many gifts of prestige given to Joseph by Pharaoh. After students have completed the sheet, briefly review the results. **What words are used to describe Joseph?** Emphasize the extent of Joseph's power. Ask a volunteer to read Genesis 41:53-57. **In the chapters that follow, the Bible records how Joseph's family was affected by the famine. They traveled to Egypt to ask for food. They ended up bowing before Joseph just as the dream had predicted so many years before. With God's help, Joseph succeeded in saving his own family as well as an entire nation! He used his authority to bring food and health to thousands.**

What qualities did Joseph need as a leader? (A strong plan for action. He needed to have confidence in the plan because some people might not have believed there would be a famine. Good organizational skills. The Bible tells us he saved so much grain they couldn't even count it!) **What would have happened if Joseph had not prepared the country for famine?** (Thousands of people would have died from starvation.) **What might have happened if the Pharaoh had refused to give his authority to Joseph?** (Everyone in the country might have starved. People might have rebelled and Pharaoh might have lost his job as ruler.) **What might have happened if the people had refused to obey Joseph's orders?** (They would not have stored enough grain. They would have starved in the famine.)

Our Bible verse for this unit reminds us that we are to obey rulers and authorities in our lives. Display the Unit Verse poster so all can see. Read the verse together aloud several times. Divide the class into several groups and give each a chance to say the verse in unison. See which group(s) can say the verse without looking at the poster.

Have you ever seen or heard about people who tie a string around their finger to help them remember something? Or maybe you've seen an ad in the newspaper telling someone to remember a sale and the ad has a picture of a finger with a string tied around it. It's an old tradition that helps give a visual reminder of something. For the next few weeks, we're going to make a booklet to remind us of God's instructions about the authorities in our lives.

Distribute one piece of construction paper to each child. Have them fold it in half to make a cover for their booklets. Encourage them to come up with original names for their booklets. Some suggestions are: "What the Bible Says About Authority," "Remember . . . ," "Who's the Boss?" Have them write the unit verse on the inside of the cover. Explain that each week they will add one more page to the booklet. Each page will tell about a way to obey and show respect for authority. As the children finish, collect the covers to use next week.

Earlier we discussed some of the leaders in our nation. Just as God chose Joseph to rule and take care of the nation of Egypt, God chooses leaders for us to follow today. Let's focus on one of those leaders who is important in our lives.

✔ Living the Lesson (5-10 minutes)

Just as the people of Egypt looked to Joseph for leadership, we look to our country's leader to provide guidance for our country. Name some of the qualities a person would need to be in charge of a nation. (Educated, fair, listens to people and their problems, good decision maker, cares for others.)

Explain that being in charge of a country is an awesome job. Any decision the leader makes affects millions of people! There are many difficult decisions to be made and people are quick to criticize if they do not agree. Refer back to the Unit Verse poster. **The first part of our verse tells us to be subject to rulers and authorities and to be obedient. But the second tells us to be ready to do good things as we follow them. One good thing we can do is to help encourage our leaders. Many people in leadership hear lots of complaints and grumbling, yet do not get much encouragement.**

Today we are going to write letters of encouragement to someone in leadership in our country. Distribute paper, pencils, and envelopes to the students. Instruct the children to write a brief note to a national or local leader, thanking him or her for being willing to be a leader. Encourage the kids to share their thoughts and ideas about leadership. They can also include a little information about your class or their own personal lives.

Collect the letters and assure the kids you will mail them this week. Close today's session by thanking God for the leaders He places in authority over us. Ask Him to help each of us to be quick to obey.

Addresses for letters:

The President
The White House
1600 Pennsylvania Avenue
Washington, D.C., 20050

Office of the Prime Minister
Langevin Block
Ottawa, Ontario K1A 0A2

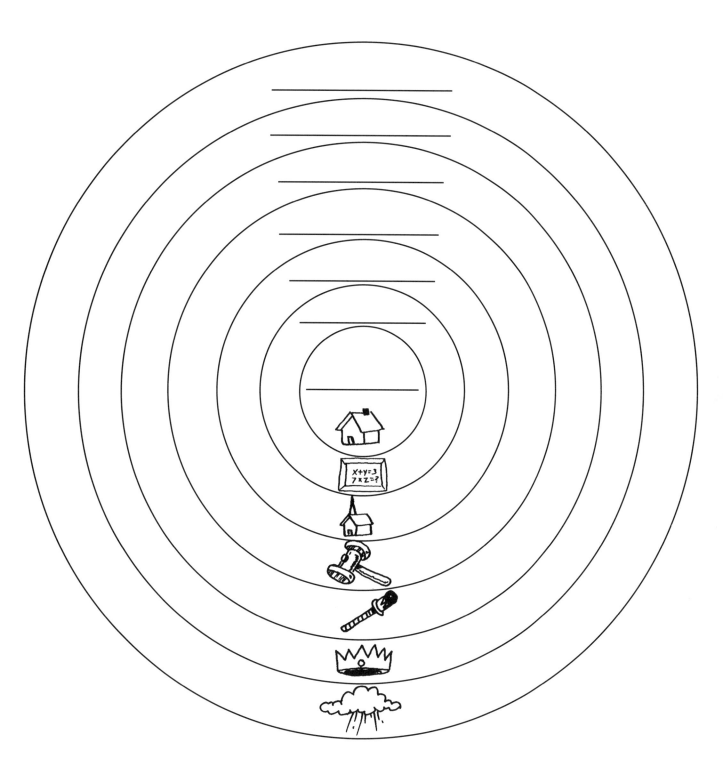

 **Pharaoh's #1 Man**

Using the pictures below, complete this verse describing the authority Pharaoh gave to Joseph.

Then Pharaoh said:

 hereby put you in of the

land of

Then Pharaoh took his signet  and put it on Joseph's

He dressed him in  of fine linen and put a gold

around his  He had him  in a

as his second–in–command, and men shouted  him, "Make way!"

Thus he put him in charge of the whole land of Egypt. Genesis 41:41-43

Lesson 2

Who's the Boss?

Aim: That your students will identify characteristics of good authorities and show respect to the authorities in their lives

Scripture: Titus 1:6-9

Unit Verse: Remind the people to be subject to rulers and authorities, to be obedient, to be ready to do whatever is good. Titus 3:1

Unit Affirmation: I CAN FOLLOW THE AUTHORITIES IN MY LIFE!

 **Planning Ahead**

1. Photocopy Activity Sheets (pages 103 and 104)—one for each student.
2. Prepare a list of the leaders in your church. Include pastor(s), staff members, and lay leaders.
3. **OPTIONAL:** Invite a lay leader or a pastor to share with the kids as described in LIVING THE LESSON.

1 Setting the Stage (5-10 minutes)

WHAT YOU'LL DO

- Lead a game of "Simon Says"

WHAT YOU'LL NEED

- A kitchen timer

2 Introducing the Issue (20 minutes)

WHAT YOU'LL DO

- Discuss the characteristics of a good leader
- Use an activity sheet to roleplay situations illustrating characteristics of good leaders
- Add a phrase to the Unit Affirmation poster

WHAT YOU'LL NEED

- "Following the Leader" Activity Sheet (page 103)
- Unit Affirmation poster

3 Searching the Scriptures (20 minutes)

WHAT YOU'LL DO

- Complete a crossword puzzle to discover what God's Word says about the traits of good leaders
- Discuss ways to show respect to authorities
- **OPTIONAL:** Create an acrostic with words that describe a good leader
- Review the Unit Verse and add a page to the Unit Verse booklets

WHAT YOU'LL NEED

- "Quality Qualifications" Activity Sheet (page 104)
- **OPTIONAL:** One or more dictionaries and a thesaurus
- Unit Verse poster and booklet covers

4 Living the Lesson (5-10 minutes)

WHAT YOU'LL DO

- **OPTIONAL:** Interview a church lay leader
- Write letters of encouragement and thanks to leaders within your church

WHAT YOU'LL NEED

- Stationery
- List of church leaders

Lesson 2

Setting the Stage (5-10 minutes)

As your class members are arriving, begin a game of Simon Says. Choose a child to be the first leader. Set a timer for thirty seconds to one minute. When the timer sounds, the current leader must pick someone else to be Simon. Repeat this process and keep the game moving with new leaders chosen continuously. Encourage as many children as possible to take a turn as leader. When a child does something that "Simon didn't say," he or she is out only for that one game. When the new leader takes over, everyone returns to the game.

> **OPTIONAL:** If the children want some variety in the game, play a different version by having the leader do a series of movements. For example, "Simon says touch toes, pat head, wiggle fingers, shake head and jump up and down." Then the group must do the same things in exactly the same order.

After all have arrived and had a chance to play, gather the group together. **Most of you had a chance to be both the leader and the player in our game. When a good leader plays Simon Says, he or she keeps you on your toes and makes it a challenge to listen closely! What characteristics of leading make it fun to follow a leader in a game like this?** Allow for responses. **Leaders in other settings have different styles of leading, too. Some are easy to follow, and others are more difficult. Today we're going to talk about those things that make it easier for us to follow the authorities in our lives.**

Introducing the Issue (20 minutes)

During our game, how many of you liked being Simon better than one of the players or followers? Why? (Fun to tell others what to do. Like being in charge. Don't have to worry about "getting out.") **How many of you did not like being the leader? Why?** (Do not like being up front. Too much pressure. Afraid of making a mistake where everyone will see.) **A good leader makes a game of Simon Says more fun. Think about all the people who led during today's game. What did they do to make it fun?** (They enjoyed the game. They were confident and excited about playing, they thought of unusual things.) **What made them easy to follow?** (They spoke loud enough for all to hear. They kept the game moving quickly. They were creative and not repetitive.)

Last week we talked about how all of us are under the authority of others.

Lesson 2 ✔

Do you remember some of the authorities we talked about? (God, world leaders, community leaders, teachers, parents.) **As we learned, we all need leaders and authorities, and they usually make our world more organized and easier to live in. But some are easier to obey and follow than others. Think about your past teachers, coaches, class officers, your parents, and your friend's parents. What qualities make some stand out as leaders who are special and above the rest?** Record their list on the chalkboard or poster board. Suggestions: fair, honest, enthusiastic, patient, easy to understand, fun, creative. **Can you think of a time when someone in authority over you was difficult to obey or follow? What made it difficult?** (Unfair and keep changing the rules, favorites get special treatment, don't care what you say or think, boring.)

    Since most of us will be leaders at some time, it is important for us to learn what makes a good leader. We also need to learn how to work with all kinds and styles of leadership. Whether it's a boss, a teacher at school or a police officer we will all have people who bug us sometimes! Distribute copies of the activity sheet "Following the Leader" (page 103) and divide the class into three groups. Assign each group one scene to act out. **In each of the scenes described on this sheet, you will find an authority who needs help! The leader has some questions and is not sure how to show strong leadership skills. Read the description of what happened and give some examples of a good leader. Prepare to present your scene for the other groups.**

    As the kids work, circulate around the room checking the progress of each group. Use the following suggestions if they need help getting started:

SITUATION #1: John could talk to an adult or other kids who are good at baseball and get help. He could choose as a co-captain someone the kids respect. The other kids can decide to be cooperative and encourage him when he does things right. The team members can work together to give some suggestions.

SITUATION #2: You could respond by talking to Mr. Benson after class to ask for more help. You could explain the effort you put into math and ask for more understanding to let Mr. Benson know how he feels and what he needs from him. Ask Mr. Benson for a suggestion of another student to help as a tutor.

SITUATION #3: You can ask for help from a teacher. You can confront the President and refuse to go along with his plan. You can follow the guidelines properly when you are in charge. If all else fails, you can resign and refuse to be a part of it.

    Invite each group to present their roleplay. Ask the following questions after each presentation: **Did you agree with the improvements made by this group? How**

were they better? What characteristics did the leader show that he or she did not before? Add any new ones to the list on the board or poster started earlier. **By studying leadership styles and skills, we can learn how to be a better follower. And, believe it or not, being a good follower is the best preparation we can have to become a good leader when it is our turn to be the authority!**

Display the Unit Affirmation poster. Ask the class to read it aloud. Think together about a phrase you could add today. Possibilities include "to learn how to be a leader myself." or "and learn what makes a good leader." **God's Word has lots to say about what makes a good leader. In fact, knowing what God expects of leaders is the best preparation for leading there is! Let's see what the Bible has to say about the characteristics of a good leader.**

✓ Searching the Scriptures (20 minutes)

It will help to have some background information about the passages for today's Scripture study. Two passages in the New Testament list requirements for church leadership, I Timothy and Titus. Both were written by Paul to struggling new churches, under the leadership of two of his dearest friends and fellow missionaries, Timothy and Titus.

Paul had left Timothy in Ephesus to help deal with some of the problems the early church was having there. First Timothy was written to give him clear instructions and encouragement. Part of his instructions included precise criteria for leadership. Titus was left in charge on Crete to organize converts there into a church. Titus was a capable and resourceful leader who had accompanied Paul on several missionary journeys. Although written to church leaders, these two letters give valuable insights into the nature of leadership and authority in any capacity. **Earlier we made a list of the qualities we thought contributed to good leadership. In the Bible, God has given us clear guidelines about the qualities that make good leaders.**

Distribute copies of the activity sheet "Quality Qualifications" (page 104). Instruct your class members to complete this crossword puzzle with words that describe leadership qualifications from the New Testament. The Scripture reference listed will give them the help they need to find the answers. Allow children to work together. Circulate around the room offering help and encouragement when needed. As children finish, begin a discussion about each of the characteristics listed. The DOWN answers are: 1-temperate, 2-self–controlled, 3-holy, 4-patient, 5-honest. The ACROSS answers are: 2-sincere, 7-hospitable, 8-example, 9-upright, 10-teach, 11-blameless, 12-gentle, 13-disciplined, 14-respectable.

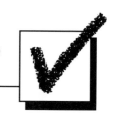

When the puzzles are complete, make a list of these words on the chalkboard or poster board, next to the list you made earlier. Then ask kids to add other qualifications listed in these passages but not included in the puzzle. They are: not quarrelsome, not a lover of money, not a recent convert, not overbearing, not given to drunkenness, manages own family well, sees that his children obey him, tested, and loyal to his mate.

This is quite a list of qualities. How are they similar or different from the list we made earlier? Allow time for responses.

OPTIONAL: To help your Juniors understand this list better, play a game to help them focus on the meaning of these words. Divide the class into teams of three or four students each. Have them write the word "Authority" in large letters across the top of a sheet of paper. Then give them five minutes to produce as long a list as possible under each letter using words that describe leadership traits that begin with that letter. They can use words from the Scripture passages, synonyms for those words, or words from the list they made earlier. They can even come up with new words, if needed. Have a dictionary and thesaurus available for use in this exercise. Examples: Under "A" they could write "accepts others' feelings" and "acts nicely;" under "U" they could write "upright" and "understanding;" under "T" they could write "teacher" and "temperate." After five minutes, compare lists. Did any teams come up with new words? Recognize the team with the longest list.

As time allows, choose several leadership characteristics to discuss further. **Why do you think this** (name a specific characteristic) **would be an important attribute for a person in authority? What problems could arise if a leader did not display this quality?** (Hurt feelings, poor example, resentment, anger, bitterness.)

No one can live up to every one of these qualifications every day of his or her life. But Paul knew that in order for the church to thrive and grow, it would need leaders who could be honest, caring examples to others. That's why he gave such detailed lists to both Timothy and Titus. Do you think a person with the qualities listed would be easy to follow or difficult to follow? (A leader of this quality would be a person others would look to as an example. Their loving attitudes and concern for others would make them easy to follow.)

Why do you think it is important for us to be talking about qualities of good leaders right now? After all, you're just kids, right? Allow kids to share their thoughts about this. Remind them of the opportunities they have to be leaders now, as illustrated on the activity page. **God knew that these qualities would take determination and practice to develop. Right now is the time for you to work on them. As adults, many of you will hold positions of authority in your school, community, or church. Begin now to ask God to help you develop these qualities in your own life!**

Display the Unit Verse poster. Say the verse together aloud several times for review. Distribute the Memory Verse booklets started last week. Be sure to have materials on hand

for those who were not present last week. Today, they will add a page to their "Reminder Booklet."

Sometimes we have trouble remembering things. That's why we create ways to remind ourselves of important things we want to be sure not to forget. What are some things we use to remind ourselves of things? (A string around our finger, a note pad, putting things out where we "trip" over them.)

God's Word says that respecting and obeying the authorities in our lives is one of those important things that is easy to forget! In fact, it is so important that we could actually put a bumper sticker on our cars or bikes as a way to remind ourselves and others to respect and obey our authorities. What are some bumper sticker slogans you've seen when riding in the car? Allow for responses. Then guide the kids to design a bumper sticker to communicate the truth of the Unit Verse. Examples might be: "Have you hugged your leader today?" "Obey is NOT a four letter word" "Rulers and authorities—God's good idea!" When they have an idea, they can draw it out on paper and include it as a page in their reminder booklets.

Bumper stickers are one way to communicate a message, but let's look at a way we can let some people know what we think in a more personal way!

☑ Living the Lesson (5-10 minutes)

End your lesson today by talking about how you can encourage and respect the leaders of your church. Take a few minutes to explain the organization and structure of your church, and possibly your denomination. Be certain the kids are familiar with the pastor(s) on staff and his (their) responsibilities. Also explain the lay leadership roles and their responsibilities.

OPTIONAL: Invite a lay leader to talk to the class about his or her role in the functioning of the church. Ask that a favorite or especially meaningful experience be shared and an explanation of the leadership responsibilities.

Use your prepared list of officers and leaders in your local congregation. Have your class write notes of encouragement to some of these leaders. Encourage them to thank the people for giving of their time, talent, and energy. Collect the cards and see that they are delivered to the proper persons.

SITUATION #1:

John has been chosen by your teacher to be one of the team captains for your class baseball game. He doesn't know much about baseball and hardly ever gets picked to be a leader. All the other kids are complaining because they don't want to be on his team. They are talking about not doing anything he tells them to do and just playing wherever and however they want.

How could John improve his leadership?

How can the rest of the kids (the followers) help him be a better leader?

SITUATION #2:

Your new teacher, Mr. Benson, is going over a new concept in math. Math has never been your best subject. It takes you a little more time and effort, but you can usually understand a new idea if you go over it a couple of times. When you asked him to review the problem again during class today, he said he didn't have time to explain. You felt stupid and embarrassed. It's only the fourth day of the school year and it's looking like this year could seem five years long!

Come up with at least two different ways to handle this problem.

SITUATION #3:

Each month, elections are held for class officers. The President and Vice President are in charge of class discipline. You have just been elected Vice President! You and the President must write the names of kids who are misbehaving on the board. The President wants to embarrass some of the kids in the class by putting their names on the board even when they don't deserve it. He also wants to protect his friends by not putting their names on the board even if they act up. He wants you to follow along with his plan.

How can you use your leadership as Vice President to handle this situation?

Quality Qualifcations

DOWN

1. MILD, MODERATE, NOT EXTREME (I Timothy 3:2)
2. THE ABILITY TO PREVENT ONESELF FROM ACTING IMPULSIVELY OR EXPRESSING STRONG EMOTION (I Timothy 3:2)
3. DEVOUT, GOD–FEARING, SINS FORGIVEN (Titus 1:8)
4. TOLERANT, NOT QUICK TEMPERED, WAITS CALMLY (Ephesians 4:2)
5. TRUTHFUL, NOT A LIAR (opposite of word in verse) (Titus 1:7)

ACROSS

2. NOT PHONY, GENUINE, TRUE, TRUSTWORTHY (1 Timothy 3:8)
7. FRIENDLY, COURTEOUS, WELCOMING TO GUESTS (I Timothy 3:2)
8. SAMPLE, STANDARD, OR MODEL (I Timothy 4:12)
9. OUTSTANDING MORAL CHARACTER (Titus 1:8)
10. WHAT AN INSTRUCTOR, TRAINER, OR EDUCATOR DOES (1 Timothy 3:2)
11. INNOCENT, GUILTLESS, WITHOUT FAULT (Titus 1:6)
12. NOT HARSH OR VIOLENT, CONSIDERATE, SENSITIVE (I Timothy 3:3)
13. RESTRAINED, USED APPROPRIATE BEHAVIOR (Titus 1:8)
14. PROPER, WORTHY OF HONOR OR RESPECT (I Timothy 3:2)

Lesson 3

To Do or Not to Do

Aim: That your students will learn that God wants us to obey authorities except in matters of personal safety or when it is against God Himself.

Scripture: Matthew 8:5-10, 13

Unit Verse: Remind the people to be subject to rulers and authorities, to be obedient, to be ready to do whatever is good. Titus 3:1

Unit Affirmation: I CAN FOLLOW THE AUTHORITIES IN MY LIFE!

 Planning Ahead

1. Photocopy Activity Sheets (pages 111 and 112)—one for each student.
2. Set up the TV studio as described in SEARCHING THE SCRIPTURE. If it is necessary to save time in class, make some of the props ahead of time.
3. **OPTIONAL:** Arrange to have a video camera, VCR and TV for your class.

 Setting the Stage (5-10 minutes)

WHAT YOU'LL DO

- Complete a word search to discover some authorities

WHAT YOU'LL NEED

- "Common Commanders" Activity Sheet (page 111)

 Introducing the Issue (20 minutes)

WHAT YOU'LL DO

- Review the importance of obeying authorities
- Play a game to discover times when it may be necessary to disobey authorities
- Add a phrase to the Unit Affirmation poster

WHAT YOU'LL NEED

- List of commands made by students
- Unit Affirmation poster

 Searching the Scriptures (20 minutes)

WHAT YOU'LL DO

- Produce a "TV Show" to explore today's Bible story
- Review the Unit Verse and add a page to the Unit Verse booklet

WHAT YOU'LL NEED

- "Good Morning Capernaum" Activity Sheet (page 112)
- **OPTIONAL:** Video camera, VCR and TV
- Unit Verse poster and Unit Verse booklets

4 **Living the Lesson** (5-10 minutes)

WHAT YOU'LL DO

- Discuss appropriate ways to influence authorities

WHAT YOU'LL NEED

- Stationery

☑ Setting the Stage (5-10 minutes)

As your students arrive today give each one a copy of the activity sheet "Common Commanders" (page 111), and instruct them to search for the words representing authorities in their everyday lives. As they find and circle each word, they are to make a list of the typical requests or commands made by that authority. (Examples: Coach—Run three laps around the field; Babysitter—Go to bed at 9:30.)

After all have arrived, gather the group together, even if the word searches aren't finished, and review their findings. As each authority is named, ask for volunteers to act out some of the requests or commands typically made by that authority. As the commands are given, record them on the chalkboard or a poster board.

How did it feel to be the authority giving the commands? Allow for responses. **How did it feel to be the ones receiving the commands?** Allow for responses. Guide your kids to talk about the fact that sometimes it feels OK to receive and obey a command, and sometimes it doesn't. **During this unit, we have been discussing how important authorities are in every person's life, and how important it is to obey the authorities. Today we want to talk about times when it might be right not to obey them.**

☑ Introducing the Issue (20 minutes)

Look over our list of commands made by these everyday authority figures. How does obeying these commands make our lives better? Allow for responses. **What would it be like if there were no parents? No teachers? No police department? Etc.?** Allow responses. **Without authorities, our world would be an unorganized, chaotic, and dangerous place to live!**

Usually instructions or requests made by authorities are made for a good reason. What are some reasons a coach might ask you to run three miles every day? (To get in shape so you have the endurance to play your best!) **What are some reasons your babysitter tells you to go to bed early?** (Your parents may have instructed him or her to do so.) **Even though it is right for us to obey the authorities in our lives, it's not always easy. Describe some times it's hard to obey someone.** (When Mom or Dad tells you to get out of bed in the morning. When a coach works you extra hard. When you have to mow the lawn and you'd rather play with friends.) **What makes it so hard to obey?** (It wasn't my idea or choice, it's hard work, I don't like doing it.)

Lesson 3

Most of the time obeying the authorities in our lives is the right, and best, thing to do. But there are times when it is O.K. and even right to disobey. Some people in authority abuse their authority. They use their power to try to get others to do things that are wrong or hurtful. There are two things you should never be forced to do. Write these two statements on the chalkboard or a poster board. YOU SHOULD NEVER DO:

#1—something that is against the laws of God or the laws of the land.

#2—something that hurts you or causes somebody else to be hurt.

What are some examples of God's laws? (No lying, no murdering, no cheating, no stealing, loving neighbors, loving enemies, living peaceably.) **What are some examples of laws of the land?** (Traffic laws, speed limits, school requirements, tax laws.) **Both God and our country made these laws for our benefit and protection. We need to obey them. If someone asks you to break one of these laws, you need to say "no" and ask an adult for help.**

What are some examples of times when you or someone else could be hurt by obeying an authority? (Treating someone else unkindly or unfairly, abusive behavior, stealing.) **When these things happen it is time for you to take a stand and say "no" to the person in authority. Thinking about what you should do in that kind of situation before it really happens will help you be better prepared if you should have to take that stand.**

Help your kids practice identifying times to say "no" by using the statements below. Read each one, instructing them to remain seated if they would obey the request and to "take a stand" (stand up) if it is something they should not obey. Ask some of the following questions after each statement. Discuss alternative actions in each situation:

• Dad tells you to take out the trash.

• Your teacher tells you it's OK to cheat on a test since it's the only way you can play on the school soccer team.

• The lifeguard at the beach tells you to come out of the water because the tides are dangerous to swimmers.

• Your baseball team is having an awful season and today's practice has been awful! Your coach gets so angry he hits one of your friends during practice. He apologizes and asks the team not to say anything to anybody about it.

• A babysitter touches you in a way that makes you uncomfortable and tells you not to tell anyone what happened.

• Aunt Marian tells you not to watch TV at her house because the baby is asleep.

• Uncle Randy takes $50.00 out of your Dad's wallet and tells you not to say anything.

Display the Unit Affirmation poster and have the class read the Affirmation aloud. Add today's phrase, "except in matters of personal safety or when it is against God Himself" to the third line. **We've spent today talking about tough decisions concerning people in authority. Let's look at a New Testament soldier who knew what good authority was all about.**

✔ Searching the Scriptures (20 minutes)

Today's Bible story will be presented as an early morning TV news program. Take time to involve all members of your class in this project.

> **OPTIONAL:** If you have access to a video camera, VCR and TV, record this news program and then watch it together.

Distribute copies of the activity sheet "Good Morning Capernaum" (page 112). Explain that in the next few minutes, you are going to turn the classroom into a TV studio and produce a TV show straight out of first–century Palestine. Begin by assigning five students to play the parts in the script and sending them to a corner of the room to practice their presentation. Meanwhile, the rest of the class will set up the "studio." You can involve them in as many of the following tasks as you have students and time to accomplish:

1. Design a logo for the TV station and draw it on a poster board. Include call letters (the initials of your church?) and a station number. Example—This is station FC (First Church), channel 39, coming to you from Capernaum, Palestine.

2. Make a sign of the show title, "Good Morning Capernaum", creating a show logo (a rising sun?) to go with it.

3. Arrange tables and chairs for "the set," including setting up the area for the audience.

4. Make "Applause" signs to be used when indicated during the interview, and assign one student to hold them up at the appropriate times.

5. Assign the other parts in the script such as: a director, a make–up person (powder the interviewers' noses prior to air time), one to four camera operators, and any others.

Stress that all must work quickly so you will have time to complete the show. After the show is completed, watch the video, if used, and then involve

Lesson 3

your students in talking about the story.

This Roman centurion had learned to operate in an environment filled with authority figures. Just like today, the military environment is filled with authority figures. Name some of the ranks within the military. (General, Admiral, Captain, Major, Lieutenant, Sergeant.) **These leaders have people under their command and they also report to those in authority over them. The centurion reported to officers with more authority than he held.**

Do you think it took courage for the centurion to go to see Jesus? Allow for responses. **What might have been some of the risks involved?** (The Roman government was concerned about Jesus and the commotion He was making. They might not have been too happy that this centurion added to the spectacle and gave Jesus more credibility. The Romans looked down on the Jews as inferior. To risk putting faith and trust in a Jewish teacher would not have been an accepted practice for a Roman officer.) **What do you think his superiors or those in authority over him might have thought?** (Some might have done the same thing. Some might have been curious about Jesus. Others might have been angry and upset.) **Did he take a chance in going to see Jesus?** (Probably.) **What things could have happened as a result?** (He might have been removed from authority because he was submitting to the authority of a Jew. If his commanders found out they might have been angry and punished him.)

In this story, we see a man who took a brave and courageous stand. He saw his servant hurt and paralyzed and risked his own position and authority to seek a higher authority—Jesus! Because of this centurion's faith, his servant was healed and Jesus was glorified!

Distribute the Unit Verse booklets from the previous week. Instruct students to open the front cover and read the verse together aloud. Ask for volunteers to say the verse on their own or in a small group. Distribute pieces of construction paper for another page in their booklets. Explain that today they will design a billboard to help people remember places and ways they can obey authority. Ask students to design and draw their billboards for the next page of the booklet. Allow students to share their completed pages with the class. Collect booklets and store them for use next week.

Over the past few weeks, we've seen the importance of obeying authorities. Today we saw how a man of faith risked his own authority by submitting to the authority of Jesus Christ. We also talked about some specific times when we need to take a stand and disobey an authority figure. Let's spend our last few minutes together today discussing how to use our authority to influence important authorities in our lives.

☑ Living the Lesson (5-10 minutes)

There's something probably each one of you have in your house that is not a person, but can be an authority if we let it. You may even have more than one. I could probably find it in most of your living rooms or family rooms, although some of you might have a smaller one in your kitchens or bedrooms. Can anyone guess what it is? (TV.)

Television programs share information, opinions, and ideas with you every day. Some of this information is good, valuable, and honors God. But some of it does not follow God's law. Name some popular shows and tell how they might not live up to God's standards. Allow for responses. What can you do to keep it from being an inappropriate authority? (Turn it off instead of watching things that don't follow God's laws, don't watch something without knowing what it is, limit your watching to just a short time.)

Are there other authorities in your life who are not being appropriate leaders? What can you do to influence them? Allow time to discuss any conflicts in authority figures.

If you know of a TV show you think violates God's laws, or an authority who isn't being a good leader, write a letter and use your influence. Ask the TV station to make some changes in their programming. Explain about the influence of a good leader. Distribute stationery and pens. After the students have signed their letters, collect them and promise to mail them during the week.

End today's session with a prayer of thanks for those in authority. Pray that leaders will obey God's laws and the laws of the land as they make decisions concerning the lives of others. Include prayer for each of your students to have the wisdom to know when to disobey the authorities in their lives.

Common Commanders

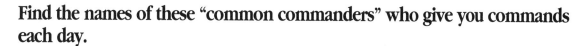

Find the names of these "common commanders" who give you commands each day.

AUNT
PRINCIPAL
UNCLE
TEACHER
POLICE OFFICER
COACH
MOM
STORE MANAGER
DAD
BABYSITTER
COUNSELOR
PASTOR
BUS DRIVER
GRANDPARENT

Write one command or instruction each of these people might give you.

```
P A S T O R B X P Y C D
Q B K B J N O L O N I A
R U M C O A C H L T Z D
Z S L A P I C N I R P X
M D X M O M Q F C K T B
G R A N D P A R E N T A
M I C F X Q U T O S M B
E V N B A K J D F B V Y
L E A Y U Q T N F T K S
C R L C N S U K I M O I
N A D X T O G T C S K T
U R E H C A E T E H A T
C O U N S E L O R M I E
S T O R E M A N A G E R
```

_____
_____
_____
_____
_____
_____
_____
_____
_____
_____
_____
_____
_____
_____

"Good Morning Capernaum"

DIRECTOR: We're on in 20 seconds.

MAKE UP: (Powders noses of stars)

DIRECTOR: And 10, 9, 8, 7, 6, 5, 4, 3, 2, 1 and Action!

STATION IDENTIFICATION: (Display station logo) This is channel 39—The one to watch!

SHOW INTRODUCTION: (Display "Good MorningCapernaum" sign) Today is (today's date). Good morning Capernaum.

(APPLAUSE APPLAUSE APPLAUSE)

HOSTESS, JOAN ENGLAND: Thank you. Good morning and welcome to Good Morning Capernaum. Today's top story: a tragic chariot accident on the main road to town. But first, let's check in with our meteorologist Fred Fairweather. How does it look Fred?

METEOROLOGIST, F. FAIRWEATHER: Well Joan, our heat wave continues with no end in sight.

JOAN: And now, back to the news. There are reports of more miracles performed by the radical Jewish rebel, Jesus. Charles Bibson has more.

CHARLES BIBSON: Thanks, Joan. We are privileged to have with us today a Roman centurion. Let's give him a warm, Good Morning Capernaum welcome!

(APPLAUSE APPLAUSE APPLAUSE)

CENTURION: Thank you, I'm happy to be here.

CHARLES: Reports say that you had a servant in your home who was very sick and in a life–threatening situation.

CENTURION: Yes, Charles, he was in awful pain and just kept getting worse. I was really afraid he was going to die.

CHARLES: So you took action. Tell our audience what you did.

CENTURION: Well, I had heard the reports of this man called Jesus. He's causing quite an uproar with all of His miracles and teachings, you know. I had heard how He had healed others and wanted Him to help my servant.

CHARLES: Weren't you afraid of what He would say? After all, you are a Roman and He is a Jew. Jews will not come to the home of a Roman because they consider us unclean.

CENTURION: I know, but I figured it was worth asking. This Jesus is not your typical, ordinary Jewish citizen. There is something special about Him! He takes command of the situation and is not afraid to make His own decisions. It was worth a try!

CHARLES: Obviously you thought so. Reports indicate that you went to Jesus asking Him to heal your servant. When He offered to come to your house you told Him that it wasn't necessary. How did you expect Him to help?

CENTURION: I am a man of authority. I report to those over me in authority and I have 100 men under my command. When I tell one of my men to "Come" he comes. When I say, "Go", he goes.

CHARLES: That still doesn't answer my question. How did you expect Jesus to help?

CENTURION: I knew Jesus had authority, even over illness. I believed that He had the power to heal my servant without actually coming to my house. He had the power and authority to do it right there on the spot, and He did!

CHARLES: That really is incredible! And I understand that Jesus was amazed by your faith. It says here He told you, and I quote, "I tell you the truth, I have not found anyone in Israel with such great faith." That's a pretty awesome statement. How does it make you feel?

CENTURION: Great! I am thrilled that my servant was healed. I believe in Jesus because he is a man of authority. I am so thankful for His willingness to help me even though I am a Roman soldier.

JOAN: Well this Jesus sure does surprise us all. Thanks for being with us today. We'll continue following the reports pouring in concerning Jesus of Nazareth. Let's pause now for a station break . . .

(APPLAUSE APPLAUSE APPLAUSE)

Head Over All Things

Aim: That your students will recognize that Jesus has all the characteristics of a good leader and deserves to be our ultimate authority.

Scripture: John 10:7-18

Unit Verse: Remind the people to be subject to rulers and authorities, to be obedient, to be ready to do whatever is good. Titus 3:1

Unit Affirmation: I CAN FOLLOW THE AUTHORITIES IN MY LIFE!

 Planning Ahead

1. Photocopy Activity Sheets (pages 119 and 120)—one for each student.
2. Prepare 30 Letter cards (approximately 4" x 4"). Write one letter on each card for the following words: PATIENT, EXAMPLE, BLAMELESS, SINCERE. Attach to the wall as described in SETTING THE STAGE.
3. **OPTIONAL:** Gather supplies to decorate the room as described in SETTING THE STAGE.
4. Wrap a medium-sized box with brown mailing paper and write the words SPECIAL DELIVERY and TO JESUS on it.
6. Draw a large outline of the number one on a poster board allowing enough room for kids' names to be signed inside the number.

 1 Setting the Stage (5-10 minutes)

WHAT YOU'LL DO

- Play a game to review characteristics of a good leader
- **OPTIONAL:** Decorate the room to look like a campaign headquarters

WHAT YOU'LL NEED

- Letter cards
- OPTIONAL: Decorating supplies

2 Introducing the Issue (20 minutes)

WHAT YOU'LL DO

- Create examples of completely trustworthy authorities and vote one into "office"
- Discuss the nature of life under untrustworthy authorities
- Complete the Unit Affirmation poster

WHAT YOU'LL NEED

- A variety of art supplies
- Unit Affirmation poster

3 Searching the Scriptures (20 minutes)

WHAT YOU'LL DO

- Use an activity sheet to list characteristics that make Jesus the #1 authority
- Review the Unit Verse and complete the booklets
- Provide an opportunity to choose Jesus as the #1 authority

WHAT YOU'LL NEED

- "Best Man for the Job!" Activity Sheet (page 119)
- Unit Verse booklets

4 Living the Lesson (5-10 minutes)

WHAT YOU'LL DO

- Write a letter to Jesus thanking Him for being their highest authority

WHAT YOU'LL NEED

- "From Me to You" Activity Sheet (page 120)
- Special Delivery Box
- Number One poster

Lesson 4

Setting the Stage (5-10 minutes)

> **OPTIONAL:** Have available a number of items to transform your room into a campaign headquarters (balloons, crepe–paper streamers, flags) Make a poster or computer banner with the phrase "Campaign Headquarters," allowing space for kids to color and decorate it. Involve any early arrivers in decorating the room to look like a political campaign headquarters.

Begin today's session by playing a game to review the qualities of good leaders. Before class, pin the letter cards to a bulletin board (or tape them to the wall) in the correct order, but with the letters facing the wall so they cannot be seen. To play, focus on one word at a time and let kids take turns guessing a letter. If the letter is in the word, turn the card(s) over so it can be read. Continue letting students take turns guessing letters until someone guesses the word. Repeat the process for each word. As children guess the answer, discuss why this quality would be important for an effective leader, and ask kids to name a few synonyms for the word. Leave the words up on the board or wall so the class can see them for the remainder of today's lesson. **We spent our first few minutes today reviewing these characteristics so you could get ready to be a campaign manager. Today we will have the opportunity to create and promote our concept of the perfect leader.**

Introducing the Issue (20 minutes)

In our country elections are held for the leaders. Many of you have probably noticed how the TV, radio, newspapers, and billboards are flooded with commercials about each candidate. These commercials are designed to convince people who to vote for. What are some other ways the candidates remind people of their names to get votes? (Bumper stickers, buttons, phone calls, banners, personal appearances.)

Briefly explain to the children how campaign managers strive to develop the perfect strategy to get their candidate elected. They design commercials to inform the public about all the reasons why their candidate is best. They work hard to get personal endorsements from influential people who can convince others of their candidate's abilities. They prepare brochures with long lists of the candidate's qualifications, experience, and goals.

Today each of you will have the opportunity to be a campaign man-

Lesson 4

ager! Divide the class into "committee groups" of two to four children. Each group must create an imaginary candidate who is running for a position of authority. The office or job isn't important. It can be King of the World, Pharaoh of Mars, Mayor, Congressman, or whatever they decide.

Explain that their campaign should be based only on the following facts. (Write these categories on a board or poster so the kids can see them as they are working.)

#1—Candidate's experience or qualifications: (List past jobs and offices along with their responsibilities.)

#2—Promises: (Make a list of promises the candidate makes to the voters.)

#3—Testimonies and endorsements of others: (Name some people and the reasons why they think their candidate would make a good authority.)

#4—Campaign Slogan: (Invent a phrase to promote the candidate. Give the class some ideas for slogans like "A kinder, gentler nation" or "Invest in a better tomorrow. Vote for...")

Provide construction paper, markers, scissors, glue, tape, and safety pins so each "committee" can make a banner and/or buttons to show support for their candidate. Instruct each group to select a spokesperson who will introduce the candidate and campaign strategy with the class. As they work, circulate among them to offer suggestions, guidance, and keep them moving.

When all have completed their tasks, give each committee one minute to present its candidate to the rest of the class. As they share, write a brief summary of each one on the board or poster including strongest attributes. After all groups have shared, hold an election to see which candidate the class likes best. Ask them to vote for the authority they would most like to obey and follow. Declare a winner and runner up.

OPTIONAL: If you have a very small class, you can work together as one group to create your idea of an ideal leader.

In creating your candidate and voting you had to make some quick evaluations and decisions. Which characteristics were most important to you? (Honesty, integrity, intelligent, fair.) **Fortunately, in our country, we have some choice in who our government leaders will be and what laws are passed. How can we make our opinions known?** (Voting, writing letters, demonstrating, campaigning for candidates.) **Voting is a very important way to have a say. When you become voting age, it will be your responsibility to research candidates and make a decision about who YOU think is best for the job. When you vote for that candidate, you are placing your confidence in that person's ability to be a good leader. We've seen in week's past how authorities can make a big difference in our everyday lives. When we follow leaders who are trustworthy, they make our lives safer and better. Unfortunately, however, not all leaders are worthy to be followed and when they are given positions of authority, life is not safe and better!**

Can you name some famous leaders in history that used their authority to abuse and hurt others? (Hitler, Saddam Hussein.) **What qualities did they have that made them poor leaders?** (Power hungry, didn't care about the people, no conscience.) **In many countries, the people have no say in who their leaders are and what laws are passed. Often they live in fear, having few freedoms. What would it be like to live under an authority that was unfair, selfish, and dishonest?** (Frustrating, frightening, scary, difficult, hopeless.) **When we think about the places in the world where people do live under this kind of leadership, we can see how important it is for us to look for good, trustworthy authorities to guide our lives!**

Display the Unit Affirmation poster and review all the statements on it. Have kids think of a statement to complete the poster. A possibility is: "when I choose them carefully!" **So far, we have been talking about human leaders in our lives. But there is only one person who deserves to be our number one authority and leader! Let's see how Jesus fills that role in our lives.**

☑ Searching the Scriptures (20 minutes)

Distribute copies of the activity sheet "Best Man for the Job!" (Page 119). **The Bible makes it clear that Jesus has all the characteristics of a good leader and deserves to be our ultimate authority. Let's look at some of His qualifications.** Instruct kids to return to their "campaign committee groups" to complete the activity sheet. They are to look up each Scripture reference and record their findings. When all have finished their research, gather them together to report. **What are some of the qualifications and significant events listed? Can you name some other events that were important during His life here on Earth?** (Possibilities are: calming of the sea, teaching, calling the disciples, feeding the five thousand, loving the unlovable.) **Which qualifications or experiences in His life are most important to you? Why?** Allow for responses.

What are some of the promises Jesus made to His followers? Unlike the politicians and leaders of our world, Jesus never breaks a promise. We can know each one of these is true and trust Jesus to do just what He says!

Candidates in political elections often use slogans to sum up their goals and objectives. Phrases like "No new taxes," or "We shall overcome," or "0% unemployment" are all short sentences that summarize their goals. Jesus used some statements to summarize the things He thought were most important. Can you name some of them? (Follow me and I will make

you fishers of men; Seek first His righteousness and all these things will be given to you; Love one another as I have loved you; I am the Way the Truth and the Life.) **Why were these important for the people to hear?**

What are some of the things people said about Jesus? (He was the Son of God, the wind and waves obeyed Him, He healed the blind and deaf.) **What are some names people used to describe Jesus? Which titles describe someone you would want to follow?** Allow for responses.

Jesus is also described as the Good Shepherd. We don't often think of a shepherd as an example of a good leader. Name some ways a shepherd is a trustworthy leader (authority) **for his sheep.** (Makes sure they have enough green grass and water; protects them from harm, especially at night when wild animals could attack; lays down his life for his sheep; nurses and cares for them when they are sick; values each sheep and will go looking for just one if it is lost.) **What are some ways we are like sheep?** (We like to go with the flock, we need protection and someone to care for us, we are lost because of our sins.) **What are some reasons why choosing to follow Jesus makes our lives better?** (He guides and protects us in all the best ways, He has laid down His life for our sins.)

In the book of John Jesus is also described as the Gate for the Sheep. That's an unusual way to describe someone. Why do you think this description was used? Allow for responses. Explain to the class how each night the shepherd rounded up his flock and put them into a pen to keep them safe from harm. Each sheep had to enter this pen through one gate. Jesus is our gate to our heavenly father. Without Jesus and His death on the cross, there would be no way for us to experience eternal life.

This is an excellent opportunity to allow your students to choose Jesus as their #1 authority. Emphasize that Jesus loves each of us so much that He wants to be our Shepherd and guide us through each day. He also described Himself as the Gate. We must walk through that Gate in order to have a relationship with God. Lead your class in a prayer thanking God for sending Jesus and providing an opportunity for your students to invite Jesus to be their #1 authority, if they have not already done so. Be sure they understand that this invitation means that they are willing to trust Jesus' leadership and follow His commands throughout their whole lives. Invite any students who make that decision for the first time today to talk with you after class or later in the week.

OPTIONAL: Involve your students in designing a campaign to promote Jesus as their #1 leader. Divide them into small groups and instruct each group to come up with a brief commercial or skit to promote their "ultimate authority"—Jesus. Their campaigns can include things like a campaign slogan (Ex-

---

amples: Things go better with Jesus. Jesus—God's #1 Choice—make Him yours!); "on–the–street" interviews (These could include the kids speaking for themselves or they can assume the role of one of the Bible characters mentioned on the activity sheet.); and campaign posters for the background. Choose activities according to the size of your class and the time available. When complete, ask each group to present their information or skit for the class.

Display the Unit Memory Verse and review it together. Remind the kids that the Bible instructs us to be obedient to rulers and authorities. **You just gave some excellent reasons and reports on why Jesus is the ultimate leader. What are some ways we can be obedient to Him?** (Read the Bible and obey its instructions. Show the same qualities as Jesus did.) Distribute paper so the students can finish their Unit Verse booklets. This week they can add a campaign button as a reminder to obey the ultimate authority—Jesus. Have the students take their booklets home this week.

✔ Living the Lesson (5-10 minutes)

Each week during this unit, we've written a letter to a different person. This week we're going to write a letter to Jesus. Distribute copies of the activity sheet "From Me to You" (page 120). Encourage students to make this a quiet time of reflection and praise. Circulate among them to offer help or suggestions, if needed. As they finish, they can tape their letters shut and deposit them into the special delivery box.

End this unit with a brief closing prayer, thanking God for giving us authorities to make life better and especially for sending Jesus to be our #1 authority.

Display the #1 poster and invite any who wish to sign his or her name inside the number one. Explain that by signing the poster, they are making an outward declaration that Jesus is #1 in their life!

Best Man for the Job!
Candidate's Name: Jesus!

Choose at least two of the verses in each category to do some research and find out more about your candidate. Write here any information that will assist you in your promotional campaign.

QUALIFICATIONS AND SIGNIFICANT EVENTS:
Matthew 4:23_____
John 2:11_____
Matthew 27:30, 31_____
Matthew 28:5-7_____

CANDIDATE'S PROMISES:
Deuteronomy 31:8_____
John 14:2, 3_____
Jeremiah 29:11_____
Philippians 4:19_____
Matthew 11:28_____

CAMPAIGN SLOGANS:
Matthew 4:19_____
Matthew 6:33_____
Mark 6:12_____
John 13:34_____
John 14:6_____

TESTIMONIES AND ENDORSEMENTS:
John 11:27_____
Mark 15:39_____
Matthew 8:27_____
Mark 7:36, 37_____

WORDS THAT DESCRIBE:
Matthew 22:16_____
Isaiah 9:6_____
John 10:7_____
John 4:42_____
John 10:11_____

From Me to You

Dear Jesus,

Just a note to let You know_____

_____

_____

_____

_____

I am thankful for_____

_____

_____

_____

My favorite way the Bible describes You is_____

_____

_____

_____

In my life, You are_____

_____

_____

_____

Signed,

_____

P. S.

Service Projects for Authority

✔ 1. Look for jobs to delegate to students in your class. Make someone responsible for taking roll one week. Have a student lead singing or review the memory verse. Interview students in front of the class asking how it felt to "be in charge" or responsible for a part of the Sunday morning experience.

✔ 2. Take a field trip. Visit a city council meeting, school board meeting, church business meeting or government building in your community. Afterward, meet together for an ice–cream snack and talk about how the business conducted helps to make life better for those in your community. Discuss what it would be like to be one of the people you saw in action.

✔ 3. Encourage some authorities by inviting them to be special guests in your classroom. Ask a police officer, a doctor, a teacher or pastor to visit your class. Ask them to describe their jobs; the parts they love and the parts they find difficult. Encourage kids to ask questions about each job and the responsibilities it entails. Before your guests arrive, invite the kids to write notes of encouragement or make cards to give at the end of the visit. Serve special refreshments as another way to say, "thanks for what you do."